MEN IN OUR TIME

MEN
IN OUR
TIME

By AUDAX (Vyvyan Adams)

Illustrated

Essay Index Reprint Series

 BOOKS FOR LIBRARIES PRESS
FREEPORT, NEW YORK

First Published 1940
Reprinted 1969

STANDARD BOOK NUMBER:
8369-1389-2

LIBRARY OF CONGRESS CATALOG CARD NUMBER:
70-99680

PRINTED IN THE UNITED STATES OF AMERICA

CONTENTS

ILLUSTRATIONS

MEN IN OUR TIME

CHAPTER I

BRITAIN AT WAR

THE American and British peoples, joint heirs of an infinitely precious heritage, are shamefully ignorant of each other. On this—the British—side of the Atlantic we see in our cinemas the shadows of American scenes and the echoes of American voices. But, as one of the tiny percentage of Englishmen who have been fortunate enough to visit your great country, I can testify that many American films are a bizarre libel on the Genuine Article.

And as for the American who has never been to England, what does the word "England" mean to him? A peaceful garden in summer, a fogbound island in winter. I am glad that this second idea is as unfair as the first is flattering. A sunny winter's day in England can invigorate like champagne. And there are parts of Britain—the industrial areas of Yorkshire, Lancashire, Scotland, and South Wales—where the pall of smoke is so constant that our famous summer has to fight a stiff battle to assert itself at all.

In these centers and in London are concentrated most of our forty-five million men and women. Over England we are packed 650 to the square mile. The British constitute a peace-loving, largely urbanized community. We are not a military nation, but we claim to be great fighters. We are deplorably easygoing. We are incredibly slow to

anger. We infuriate friend and foe alike by our reluctance
to feel insulted. We enter a quarrel with heavy feet. Yet,
once in, we can be stubborn.

In this book some mention is made of our recent naval,
military, and air efforts. All three are already formidable;
before long they will be terrific. But I am not setting out
to describe material achievement or military endeavor.
My purpose is to depict the characters of the men on
whom now rests the supreme political responsibility of
directing the British war effort. That responsibility is
today concentrated in a few hands. So first I ask and seek
to answer the question: Why is that concentration deemed
the best plan in this war of siege, darkness, and surprise?

"The British always lose every battle except the last
one." Great Britain's history has largely justified this gibe
—or this tribute. There have been exceptions, the most
famous being the War of American Independence. But
by and large, and always when her own national independence is at stake, Britain *does* prevail in the final stages
of wars. The last battle is the battle to win.

That is a comforting reflection to foster when days are
dark or progress is slow. But it does not imply the highest
praise for British efficiency. Must we always, it may be
asked, move so slowly into action that nine battles have to
be lost before we win the decisive tenth? Britain has a
long history of the experience and endurance of reverses.
In the First German War we saw the territory of ally after
ally overrun. Serbia, Belgium, Rumania, and large parts
of France, Russia, and Italy were submerged. In the outlying campaigns in Africa and Asia Minor we did have
some successes before the final months. But most of the
campaign was for us a tale of vigilance and fortitude, and
of the loss by Britain of nearly one million dead, till the

eventual sudden victory on the western front of the American, French, and British armies.

The same was true of a far smaller affair—the South African War against the Boers at the turn of the present century. It certainly resulted in the addition of great territories to the British Commonwealth, territories quickly formed into a self-governing dominion. It was hardly more than a painful incident fought by a tiny fraction of the total British man power. Yet its early stages were marked by reverses and disasters. The plan of campaign was muddled and the pertinacity of the Boers was at first sadly underrated. In my chapters on Eden and Churchill this unhappy conflict will be mentioned again. I refer to it here as an instance of our character for muddling through catastrophe to great success.

The Zulu War, in the late seventies of the nineteenth century, and the Indian Mutiny and the Crimean War, in the fifties, were all distinguished by calamity or mismanagement. In 1879 at Isandhlwana a horde of black warriors cut to pieces a British force of 1,300 men. But at Rorke's Drift about a hundred Englishmen behind a barricade of biscuit boxes held a vital position for nearly twelve hours against 4,000 Zulus. On July 4th of the same year the native leader Cetewayo was finally defeated by Lord Chelmsford at Ulundi.

As for India, who has not heard of the massacre of Cawnpore and the defense of Lucknow? As for the Crimea, Florence Nightingale was immortalized by her fight against the frightful hospital conditions that prevailed there till her intervention. Yet all these campaigns eventually added luster to the British flag.

Thus, I could continue the tale of early defeat converted into final victory for Britain. Most pertinent of all

were the long Napoleonic campaigns; we did not lose
Waterloo.

In this war in which we are now engaged the British
government has shown from the start that it intends to
avoid the mistakes of the past. It was only at a comparatively late stage of the Great War that Lloyd George, on
succeeding Asquith as prime minister at the end of 1916,
hit upon the arrangement of concentrating the supreme
direction of affairs in the hands of a War Cabinet containing only five members. They were Lloyd George, the
prime minister, Bonar Law, chancellor of the exchequer,
Arthur Henderson, the Labor leader, and Lord Milner—
"Ministers without Portfolio," and Lord Curzon, lord
president of the council. Later General Jan Smuts, our
ex-enemy from South Africa, was admitted.

Of the original members, Lloyd George is left alive. At
seventy-seven he is the most vital human dynamo I know.
I wish I could write at length of him, but he is outside the
pattern of this book.

The secretary of that War Cabinet was Sir Maurice
Hankey. The foreign secretary, Mr. Balfour, could claim
access to it whenever he desired.

Normally a Cabinet in Britain consists of about twenty
individuals. Each member, except the prime minister,
the lord chancellor, the lord privy seal, and the lord president of the council, has a salary of $25,000 a year. The
first two of the exceptions receive $50,000 each. The other
two get $15,000 apiece.

For great emergencies and quick decisions such a Cabinet of twenty is clearly too cumbrous. Chamberlain has
compromised between Lloyd George's Cabinet of five and
the normal peacetime number by setting up a Cabinet of
nine. Nine character studies of British leaders are con-

tained in this book, but two of them are not in the War Cabinet. Mr. Duff Cooper has today no office at all; he is merely a private member of the House of Commons. Mr. Anthony Eden, the dominions secretary, like Balfour, the foreign secretary in the last war, while not a member of the War Cabinet, may enter it whenever necessary. Indeed, I understand he is working in it for most of every day. The same is true of Sir John Anderson, the home secretary.

There are then two members to whom I am not allotting separate chapters. They are Lord Hankey (the former Sir Maurice Hankey) and the minister for the co-ordination of defense, the sailor Lord Chatfield.

Hankey is a confidential encyclopedia. His position is almost as valuable as that of a constitutional monarch; for he also is steeped in precedent, and so long and unbroken has been his service as secretary to the highest councils that he is able to defeat or carry a proposition by saying what was done in similar circumstances twenty years ago or more.

The career of this remarkable man may be sketched in a few sentences. Hankey was born in 1877, joined the marine artillery in 1895, and served in the Naval Intelligence Department from 1902 to 1906. Without any kind of self-assertion he was soon recognized as a brain of a quality that occurs but rarely in each generation. He made the perfect confidential secretary to whom secrets of vast moment were as private as his own heart.

In 1912 he was secretary of the Committee of Imperial Defense; Lloyd George made him secretary of the War Cabinet in 1916. From 1919 to 1938, although the government changed several times, he remained as secretary to the Cabinet. He has, moreover, been secretary to the

following conferences: the Imperial Conferences of 1921,
1923, 1926, and 1930; the Peace Conference of 1919; the
Washington Naval Conference of 1921; the Genoa Conference of 1922; the Reparations Conference in 1924; the
Hague Conference of 1929-1930; the London Naval Conference of 1930; and the Lausanne Conference in 1932!
Never in British history has there been a more complete
instance of "the hand behind the throne."

It was his business to know everything and to remember
everything but to publish nothing. For over a quarter of
a century he enjoyed unparalleled power as an adviser,
but not as an executive. Thus, wielding a singular discretion, he could even make and unmake ministers. Nobody
indeed was better able to judge what individuals and
what combinations would best serve the state.

In 1914 it was feared that the Germans might invade
our south and east coasts. Upon Hankey among others
fell the work of organizing the civil population for such a
contingency. All through the First German War he had to
be ready with reports of the situation in all theaters of
war and with outlines of plans for future strategy.

One of the men who most valued Hankey's services was
Lord Balfour. Hankey actually supervised the personal
comfort of the chief British delegate to the Washington
Naval Conference in 1921. In England, Balfour used a
special type of long envelope for the notes of his speeches.
He was meticulous about such things as this, and thought
that no similar envelopes would be found in America.
Hankey found them for him.

But his services far exceeded such amusing trivialities.
No mere "gentleman's gentleman" is Lord Hankey. Bal-
four once observed in private conversation with a friend,
"I tell you that without Hankey we should not have won

The commanders of England's "home front"—the British War Cabinet and Ministers who have access to the Cabinet. *Left to right, standing*—Sir John Anderson, Minister for Home Security; Lord Hankey, Minister Without Portfolio; Leslie Hore-Belisha, former Secretary of State for War (this position is now held by Oliver Stanley); Winston Churchill, First Lord of the Admiralty; Sir Kingsley Wood, Secretary of State for Air; Anthony Eden, Secretary of State for Dominion Affairs; Sir Edward Bridges, Secretary to the War Cabinet. *Left to right, seated*—Lord Halifax, Foreign Secretary; Sir John Simon, Chancellor of the Exchequer; Neville Chamberlain, Prime Minister; Sir Samuel Hoare, Lord Privy Seal; Lord Chatfield, Minister for Co-ordination of Defense.

the war." Later on, when his confidant reminded him of this dictum, Balfour exclaimed, "Well! I don't think I exaggerated!"

Hankey's genius consists of an effortless capacity for taking infinite pains. Within the head of this one man is stored a wealth of knowledge and deep confidences. And he enjoys more than the confidence of his eminent contemporaries and superiors; he enjoys their friendship as well.

Yet he is virtually unknown to the general British public whose rulers he has served so long and so efficiently. To most of us he remains a dim figure with an enormous intellect. This frail man walks along Whitehall almost completely unrecognized by passers-by, his placid gray eyes fixed upon some remote horizon. A puff of wind might waft away Lord Hankey into some intellectual stratosphere. But to his colleagues he is a tower of strength, a counselor who is nearly infallible.

The other member of the Cabinet whom I shall not describe at length is Lord Chatfield. Aged sixty-six, he is that rare phenomenon in Britain—a sailor who can deliver a speech as effectively as he can handle a battleship. In this, he ranks with another successful talker among distinguished sailors whom I have heard, the American Admiral William S. Sims. Chatfield has intellectual force too. Even in that exclusive section of peers who regularly debate in the House of Lords he is fully able to hold his own.

Chatfield has the necessary breadth of mind to co-ordinate the activities of the three services, yet he should be celebrated as a great naval commander. He knows war at first hand. All through the First German War he served immediately under Admiral Beatty as his flag captain. He was in action at Helgoland, the Dogger Bank, and Jutland.

Possibly the British public knows him best for the historic order received from Beatty at Jutland. Beatty had his admiral's flag on Chatfield's ship, the *Lion*. In the preliminary stages of the action, with his squadron of six battle cruisers he had a numerical superiority over the German Admiral Hipper's five battle cruisers. But within half an hour Beatty's superiority of one became an inferiority of four against five. For the *Indefatigable* was blown up by the marvelous German gunfire and the *Queen Mary*, through the same terrific agency, caught fire, capsized, and exploded.

The *Lion* herself, containing Admiral Beatty and Captain Chatfield, was struck and one of her turrets caught fire, threatening the magazines. But Beatty, now at a numerical disadvantage, continued to press the Germans.

Suddenly an enemy salvo descended around the *Princess Royal*, the battle cruiser next astern of the *Lion*. She was momentarily shrouded in spray and smoke. A signalman appeared on the bridge of the *Lion* and said, *"Princess Royal* blown up, sir." Beatty snapped to his flag captain, "Chatfield, there seems to be something wrong with our —— ships today. Turn two points to port!"

Even Winston Churchill, who seldom shrinks from picturesque language, and who records this incident in his war memoirs, is unable to record in writing the lurid adjective which qualified Beatty's reference to the vast sea castles under his command. But every British layman appreciates the suicidal nature of the order that Chatfield had to carry out. "Turn two points to port" meant two points nearer the German battle cruisers. The four—apparently three—surviving British battle cruisers were, it might be imagined, being driven into the jaws of death.

In fact, this daring movement saved the day. Within minutes Beatty and Chatfield had the satisfaction of seeing our guns, at the shorter range, begin to prevail against the enemy, the accuracy of whose fire began to deteriorate. And Chatfield can look back with satisfaction on his important share in what may have been a turning point of naval history. After Jutland the German High Seas Fleet emerged only once—to surrender to Beatty.

By 1933 Chatfield had risen to be the professional head of his service by becoming first sea lord and chief of the Naval Staff. He reached the highest rank in the navy— "Admiral of the Fleet"—in 1935. In 1937 Admiral of the Fleet Sir Ernle Chatfield was made first Baron Chatfield. In 1938 his term as first sea lord was ended, but by the end of that year the skies had begun to grow black enough for Chamberlain to replace the ex-attorney general, Sir Thomas Inskip, by the sailor Chatfield as minister for the co-ordination of defense.

Chatfield and Hankey are members of the House of Lords. They have spent none of their lives in the more powerful and vital limb of Parliament—the House of Commons. In one important respect the British practice differs from the American. There is in England a convention that is seldom dishonored—each member of the Cabinet must be in one of the Houses of Parliament. So, if a prime minister needs in his government one or more men of outstanding capacity who have had no parliamentary experience he may elevate them to the peerage, when they will automatically sit in the House of Lords.

But most of our political leaders are recruited from the House of Commons. Indeed, the constitutional theory is that anyone is entitled to be prime minister who can command a majority in Commons. Political democracy has thus a very real meaning in Great Britain.

Do we or do we not get the leaders we need? On the whole, this method of finding ministers has served us well. Before the First German War we had a Liberal prime minister, Mr. Asquith, a monumental figure, conceivably a greater man as a peacetime administrator than his dynamic successor. But during his administration we had to go to war. After two years it seemed that the campaign was not being conducted with the necessary resolution, so Asquith was succeeded by a man who is perhaps the greatest political figure alive in the world today—David Lloyd George.

Perhaps no other man than Lloyd George could have rallied the national effort in the darkest days of the last war. As minister of munitions, he got the guns. He produced the shells. And when, after he became prime minister, the perverse conservatism of some of his colleagues and subordinates resisted new methods of dealing with the enemy at sea he insisted upon them and so saved Britain from starvation.

Great services—yielded by a great man. And how was the greatness discovered in this nonconformist Welsh solicitor, wholly without the initial advantages of birth, wealth, or education? It flashed out in the rough-and-tumble of democratic politics both outside and, more markedly, within the chamber of the House of Commons.

Lloyd George's exciting premiership ended as long ago as 1922. He was succeeded by a man whose great and serene qualities could have found their scope only in the House of Commons—Mr. Bonar Law. He won a general election on the strange slogan "tranquillity." After illness took him out of public life, we had Mr. Stanley Baldwin, a recent discovery of Bonar Law's from among the ranks of Conservative "backbench" members of the House of Commons.

Then there was Ramsay MacDonald, a man whose humble birth was no bar to his winning the position of first Labor prime minister largely through the thunder and lightning of his rhetoric and through his skill as a parliamentarian. For some time MacDonald heightened the color of British politics as Lloyd George had done. The next prime minister was Baldwin again (1924-1929). MacDonald again (1929-1931). Then a coalition between them after the financial crash, with MacDonald continuing as titular prime minister. Then Baldwin from 1935 to 1937. That brings us to the present prime minister, Neville Chamberlain.

He is going to be described in considerable detail. But he is seventy and may need a successor before we have won this war. Who is that likely to be?

I regard two possibilities among several as the most probable—Lord Halifax and Winston Churchill. The claims of Halifax depend largely on his record as viceroy of India and as foreign secretary, and on an almost saintly spirituality of character. And even he began his public career with long service in the "Lower House."

As for Winston Churchill, he is the supreme performer of the present century in the House of Commons. Make no mistake about this—Winston puts the claims of the House before all else. He knows it is the ideal sounding board for his magnificent oratory. Before the elected representatives of the British people he feels it his duty to deliver his most brilliant periods and to unfold his own tremendous ideas of policy. Although he has sat in it for so great a total of years he treats this assembly with the respect due to one's mother.

If, in the pages which follow, you find scenes and speeches in Parliament constantly asserting themselves, you are asked to remember that the House of Commons is more than the Mother of Parliaments. It is the center of our public life, the nursery and magnet of our great political figures.

Physical violence rarely intrudes into Parliament. And the debates of peace are different from the violence of war. Yet they both require some of the same qualities—courage, patience, hard hitting, pugnacity, resolution. I do not believe that the parliamentary politician need prove a timid or undecided wartime minister. In any event the normal asperities of party politics are suspended during this period of war. The government's foe is Hitler, not His Majesty's Opposition.

We are ready to face a long war, and there may be many changes in the personnel of our government before the "cease fire" is sounded. There is no coalition today. The Opposition criticize with vigor and effect. Parliament—both government and Opposition sides—has insisted on some modification of the wartime restrictions and regulations.

In this book little mention is made of the more prominent figures in the Opposition or among the younger politicians still in their thirties. Indeed, many of these last are in the services. But from these two reservoirs must be drawn the streams of fresh ministerial talent when the grip of the older men begins to relax.

I think a coalition in Britain is a lively probability before the end of hostilities. Then those citizens of the United States who are interested in Britain's destiny will

have to accustom themselves to a new set of names of
which they have so far hardly heard—Arthur Greenwood,
Sir Archibald Sinclair, Major Clement Attlee, Herbert
Morrison, and so on.

All the men described in the following chapters are
more or less well known to me personally. They are all
admirable in greater or less degree. They are all resolute
for the triumph of tolerance over tyranny. But they are
all human. A version of this book is now on sale in Britain.
It has been received more kindly than its author had expected. Democracy, praise heaven, recognizes that nobody, however eminent, has ever been injured by a little
friendly iconoclasm. The political leader can and should
be revealed as a human being. Even in times of war democratic statesmen are as human as they were before the
temporary exile of peace. No supermen for us!

CHAPTER II

NEVILLE CHAMBERLAIN
The Man with the Umbrella

MILLIONS of men and women in Europe now have their normal occupations broken by the wail of the sirens presaging death, fire, and mutilation from the skies. Such, it might be said, is not an easy moment to write objectively. Yet gratitude and compassion ultimately dominate my feelings as I approach the character of one of the most famous figures in the world, the man who made inevitable the downfall of Nazidom—Mr. Neville Chamberlain.

I feel gratitude because he led the British Commonwealth of Nations into war against the most evil of all tyrannies. Though that action may mean that I, as well as millions of others, may not live to see triumph the cause which Great Britain will not allow to fail, I thank him for recognizing that there are evils fouler than war. Without freedom and the assurance of honorable dealings in the affairs of nations, we are better dead. Vindicate those principles, even at the cost of many lives of happy performance or of glowing promise, and life again is fit to be lived by adult men and women.

I write of Neville Chamberlain the man as much as of Neville Chamberlain the statesman. After Munich he said that he and his colleagues would carry with them to the end of their days the marks of what they had endured.

And he was right. During the last two years age has begun to challenge his fiber, yet he is still a man whose whole body suggests the qualities of iron. His prevailing color is iron-gray. Till very recent years his head was covered with jet and orderly hair. It is as plentiful as ever but time has touched him. He is gray at the temples and above the forehead, so that in the distance he might appear to have a chaplet fitted on his brow. His eyebrows and mustache also are streaked with white.

Yet Chamberlain's physique gives the lie to his age. Crises and long hours may sometimes wither his face with fatigue but, after a rest, and when the demands of disturbance are keeping down their heads, he carries his thin frame as briskly as a man in the middle fifties. In March, 1939, just after the Munich appeasement had been finally dissipated by Hitler's sudden absorption of the remainder of Czechoslovakia, Chamberlain completed seventy years of life. He is justly proud of his youthfulness. Like some other young men, he has shown himself able to learn.

Eminence often means loneliness. And even for so eminent a man, Chamberlain is one of the loneliest figures I have ever known. He has the Englishman's reserve developed to a point which shuts him off from the world and deters those who, with the most excellent motives, wish to get near to him. Yet this detachment is a superficial thing. He is a happy and devoted husband. In public he typifies his countrymen in their loathing for any emotional demonstration. Yet once, when introducing a bill into the House of Commons, dealing with maternity services, his hearers were astonished to see him come to the edge of tears as he referred to his own mother's death when he was born.

Possibly as a mere diversion, more likely as a device to penetrate his austerity, young men have tried to find a nickname for the prime minister. The cult of the Christian name now current among politicians in England seems inadequate. Not many of the suggestions are suitable. Here are a few of them—supported by explanatory notes:

"The Housemaster" is employed by those who, at half his age, have found it difficult on social occasions to forget the discipline of party. The restraints and discomforts of school have reasserted themselves.

The next is "The Clothesbrush"—you see the prickly personality and the wiry mustache. This is one of the poorer suggestions. So for fresh inspiration they turn, as others have done when faced with a problem of comparable gravity, to the farmyard. They say that when his jaw drops and he looks up in momentary perplexity he deserves to be called "The Hen." Certainly there is a colorable similarity.

Or they call in aid from the treetops and choose a fowl of darker plumage and more ominous significance. Neville Chamberlain becames "The Crow." One dignified critic called him "corvine rather than aquiline." That is not so bad. He insists on wearing the kind of funereal garb that covers an undertaker. His long black coat, black shoes, and dark tie seem to demand the complement of black gloves and a top hat with the broadest possible band of mourning.

Another essay along the same line, for which far higher credit is due, is "The Coroner." You feel that at any inquest he could be trusted to detect any irregularity of death or violence suffered by the deceased. He would take a pride in doing his grim task with thorough efficiency.

The melancholy in his voice would be appropriate to his findings. "The Coroner," then, must be set high among these somewhat unsatisfying ventures.

It is far better than "The Scarecrow." Lean and formidable Chamberlain probably is, but he does not invite anything like such a repulsive description. Blasphemous, but pointedly ironical, is "The Prince of Peace"; in any case, it could not be made to stick, so it misses the first requirement in a nickname.

On the whole, first prize should go to "The Winged Ironmonger." It takes rather long to say, but it does succeed in compressing within a small compass a multitude of ideas. His belated exploits as an aeronaut and all that they portended for the blessing and the cursing of mankind are at once recalled. "Ironmonger" is masterly. The background of Birmingham, the sovereign center of commercial ironmongery in Britain, springs before the mind's eye.

Unlike Stalin, Chamberlain is not to be identified with steel. The metal that he purveys is in an earlier and more malleable condition. Tough it may be, but not so tough that it will not bend, with or without being raised to a red glow, after a few stout strokes from a hammer. In some forms and in limited quantities iron may even be taken as a medicine. One has yet to hear of a patient willingly swallowing steel.

When you are within a yard of Chamberlain you will revise your first impression. The thinness of body is just as marked as at a greater distance, but the face must belong to someone who has been through the fires of great anxiety. Political friends lament the certainty that he cannot lead much longer. Lloyd George was a mere fifty-nine when he was deposed. Ramsay MacDonald retired at sixty-eight. Baldwin stepped into the shadows when he was just short of seventy. It is no use to point to Gladstone. Chamberlain may possess some of Gladstone's inner fires to impel him forward, but the burden of supreme responsibility is today too heavy for any man to sustain for long after he has reached three score years and ten.

The war has upset all electoral calculations. Friends and foes who assumed that circumstances would allow of a general election before October, 1940, could treat it as virtually certain that he would not last as prime minister beyond the middle of the life of the next Parliament. At this moment I presume to offer no verdict upon his work, and these words are not intended to bear more than their face value: no man has undergone a more fearful strain; he deserves a rest. May his physique be as enduring as it seems so that he may long enjoy it.

To some he has seemed a strangely municipal figure. The late Lord Birkenhead is credited with a characteristic pronouncement upon him: "He would make a good town clerk of Birmingham in a bleak year." Except when he is enjoying the relaxation of fishing, he wears the wing collar now seldom worn in daylight except by members of the legal profession.

Chamberlain seems fashioned to endure the rigors of winter as well as to enjoy the exuberance of summer. Beyond a doubt he is a big man. Some of his admirers have called him "great." If that is so, one quality more than any other elevates him to that level. It is his moral courage. On some men it confers weakness as well as strength and has been known to breed obstinacy and self-satisfaction. In Chamberlain the quality is there in full measure wrought into the iron of his constitution. In the vulgar language of a facetious young critic, "I'm bound to say the old boy's got guts."

During the last half century three Chamberlains have been in the forefront of British public life. Of the three, Neville seemed in his early years least likely to rise to be the head of a government. But for Home Rule, Joseph, the father, might have succeeded the Liberal prime minister, Gladstone. But for the issue of tariffs, he might have displaced Balfour, the Conservative prime minister. At the age of seventy he was suddenly struck out of public life by ill-health and lingered in the twilight for eight more years.

On two occasions at least, perhaps on three, Austen, Neville's elder half brother, seemed within an ace of the Conservative leadership. Scrupulous honor and studious self-effacement held him back. Yet here was a man who seemed clearly marked out to be prime minister. At the age of forty he was chancellor of the exchequer. Neville, who has reached an eminence above the high-water mark of either of the others, did not even enter Parliament till he was nearly fifty. This he did at the general election of 1918.

He had had an earlier and unfortunate taste of administration when he was suddenly appointed director-general of national service by Lloyd George as soon as he became prime minister at the end of 1916. The National Service Department was intended to form a pool of volunteer labor from which workers could be drafted into different parts of industry as and when they were needed. This ambitious plan succeeded only in causing friction and discontent. Neville Chamberlain, who had resigned the lord mayoralty of Birmingham to undertake the work, threw up the new office after seven months. This failure was not his fault. Nor was an earlier experience of frustration when his father had sent him to the West Indies for seven years to plant sisal, the West Indian fiber plant. The sisal plants rusted at the moment when they should have begun to be profitable. Joseph Chamberlain lost a fortune in the venture. But neither this private failure nor the public inefficacy of the National Service scheme was the fault of Neville. Any blame for the first must be laid to Joseph, for the second to the grandiose energies of Lloyd George. That is admitted; but one wonders if his participation in the mistakes of others did not begin to endow Neville with a conviction of personal infallibility. He might be tempted to say to himself, "Things have a way of going wrong, but it is never my fault."

His name was worth gold in the Conservative party. After the defeat of Germany, English parliamentary representation touched its nadir. One observer said the House of Commons that came in on the 1918 elections was "full of seedy company promoters." Another said many of its members were "hard-faced men who looked as though they had done well out of the war." Lloyd George said that when he faced the Opposition he might be looking at the Trades-Union Congress. He added that when he turned round to his own side he saw the Federation of British Industries. Such an atmosphere might delay the most promising growth.

But, when the Conservative-Liberal Coalition split and Sir Austen Chamberlain went into retirement with Lloyd George, Bonar Law made Neville in turn, between October, 1922, and May, 1923, postmaster general, paymaster general, and minister of health. Bonar Law retired to fade sadly away into the grave. Baldwin succeeded and raised

Neville Chamberlain into the vacant office of chancellor of the exchequer.

So, after four years and a half of parliamentary experience he was promoted to an office whose occupant is theoretically the prime minister's first lieutenant. He preferred the chance to accomplish good work to the business of making himself famous. After the Conservative victory at the end of 1924, when Winston Churchill became chancellor, Chamberlain went back without regret to the Ministry of Health. The officials there found him a good minister to work for.

His name and prestige were growing within the party, and he began to seem the most probable successor to Stanley Baldwin. He had always been wedded to the policy of tariffs and he now saw before him the opportunity of reintroducing his father's policy, which the country had rejected a quarter of a century before. During the three short months of the emergency National administration of 1931 he returned once more to the Ministry of Health, but he was not to stay there long. His is said to have been one of the most insistent voices in favor of an early general election.

After the election the Conservative party in the House of Commons started a vehement clamor for protection—even before MacDonald had determined the personnel of his government. Who would become chancellor of the exchequer in succession to the suddenly ennobled Viscount Snowden? The Tory hosts were somewhat mollified and reassured by seeing the key office go to Neville Chamberlain.

In his own sphere Chamberlain now became an autocrat. For nearly six years he managed the country's finances with great shrewdness. No one can say that, accord-

ing to the standards he set himself and within the limits
of his office, his stewardship was anything but a success.
Only at the end did he seriously stumble over his first
complicated scheme for the National Defense Contribution. It proved so distasteful to the Conservatives in 1937
that it had to be withdrawn and replaced by a simpler
scheme for which his successor Simon took responsibility.

After the ballot boxes had yielded up their secrets in
November, 1931, the foreigner was tempted to increase
the dumping of cheap manufactured goods on to the
British market to anticipate any permanent protective
legislation that might follow. A measure bearing the
dreadful title of "The Abnormal Importations Customs
Duties Bill" was hustled through Parliament to prevent
forestalling. By the early days of February Chamberlain
had got his way. Certain dissentient Liberal ministers
headed by Sir Herbert Samuel were allowed to stay in the
Cabinet by a notorious—and, for England, unprecedented
—"agreement to differ." The theory of English cabinets
is that each and every member shall be individually responsible for the Cabinet's collective decisions.

The cumbrously worded act was superseded by the
Customs Duties Bill. Chamberlain's moment had come.
In proposing the tremendous reversal in the House of
Commons, he said, "I do not think that any reasonable
man would say that the delay has been unduly protracted.
Barely three months have passed since the most remarkable election in the whole of our political history—" A
certain Labor member—now dead—interrupted loudly,
"And the most corrupt!" Chamberlain looked up in momentary surprise. He seemed startled, but not afraid. He
did not bother to retort to his heckler, but proceeded to
state his case with exemplary clarity.

British Combine Photo

Neville Chamberlain, Prime Minister, and Lord Halifax, Secretary of State for Foreign Affairs, discuss the uncertainty of Europe's future from the equally uncertain deck of a cross-channel steamer. It is yet too early to predict whether or not Chamberlain is the man who has made inevitable the downfall of Nazidom, but there is no doubt that he is the leader of England's fight in fact as well as in name. Lord Halifax, good naturedly known as "The Holy Fox," is a veteran of many diplomatic engagements and a stubborn fighter whose decisions are based on a deeply spiritual evaluation.

He summarized under seven heads the expectations which he and his colleagues entertained about the new policy. They are well worth reading in an abbreviated form: They hoped to correct the balance of payments; to raise fresh revenue to maintain the value of our currency and to prevent a rise in the cost of living; to bring to British industry and agriculture work then being done abroad; to make methods of production more efficient; to arm Britain with an instrument for bargaining; to promote imperial preference and so to strengthen the ties of imperial unity.

He spoke for an hour and a quarter and, in the same toneless voice, ended with a finely fashioned tribute to his father: "His work was not in vain. Time and the misfortunes of the country have brought conviction to many who did not feel that they could agree with him then. I believe he would have found consolation for the bitterness of his disappointment if he could have seen that these proposals, which are the direct and legitimate descendants of his own conception, would be laid before the House of Commons which he loved, in the presence of one and by the lips of the other of the two immediate successors to his name and blood."

He sat down beside the president of the Board of Trade. Runciman of the inscrutable features actually smiled and patted him twice between the shoulder blades. From any Englishman in an important position this gesture is almost riotous; coming from the sphinxlike Runciman, it was staggering. Sir Austen Chamberlain rose from his seat on a back bench, took off his top hat, and proceeded to the Front Bench where he silently and solemnly shook his half brother by the hand.

This moment was for Neville a real, an abiding triumph. A far more violent demonstration of enthusiasm accompanied the end of his speech on Wednesday, September 28, 1938, just before the Munich conference, but on that occasion many members could not have said whether they were cheering Chamberlain or Providence. On February 4, 1932, the acclamation was exclusively for Neville Chamberlain.

While chancellor of the exchequer, he introduced six budgets. The unemployed had their full benefits restored to them and in course of time all the other cuts inflicted at the financial crisis in 1931 were healed. Up to the moment of his introduction of the National Defense Contribution, employment steadily rose to unprecedented levels. He hardly expected or measured his own success. During the darkest period of unemployment, when asked how long he expected the problem to remain acute, he said with colorless candor, "Ten years." This honest pessimism was so outspoken that the storm of taunts which it raised quickly died away.

Now, this background of municipal experience and administrative success was hardly the best possible training for the handling of foreign affairs. He took a few stabs at them before he became prime minister. Early in this period as chancellor of the exchequer he made a speech at a public dinner in which he warned the American administration of the dangers of overspending. He excused this unusual course in this way: it could hardly be an unfriendly act for him to shout out a warning to a friend who was walking along the edge of a precipice!

But his three steps that are deepest in the memory are associated with Italy. When he first grasped the full meaning of Italy's projected aggression against Ethiopia and the threat it implied to British interests, he and Lord

Hailsham were most zealous for strong measures. After the election of 1935 he failed to grasp the grievous thing that M. Laval and Sir Samuel Hoare had done by making their Paris proposals. At first he and his colleagues in the Cabinet endorsed Hoare's action; then, when the storm arose inside and outside Parliament, they repudiated him. Hoare resigned.

At the end of the debate on Hoare's resignation Chamberlain wound up for the government. Early in his speech he said with a really alarming frankness, "I say for myself that, though I recognize today that that decision [i.e., to back the Laval-Hoare proposals] was a mistake, *I cannot say that in similar circumstances I should not again commit that mistake.*" So it was on a man thus "moving about in worlds not realized" that the League and collective security were to depend for their survival.

In June, 1936, Chamberlain distinguished himself even more brightly in pastures strange to him. Lord Cecil had made a speech urging the continuance and, if possible, the strengthening of League sanctions against Italy. Mr. Chamberlain was the chief guest at the dinner of the 1900 Club. He was there in the company of Lord Londonderry, Mr. Winston Churchill, and other shining lights of Conservatism. It was not an important occasion and the company of men and women were expecting a fairly festive evening. Winston Churchill did what was expected of him. He made an amusing speech contrasting the outlook and habits of 1900 with those of 1936. But Neville Chamberlain took it upon himself to use this occasion for a sharp retort to Lord Cecil. After referring to Italy's flagrant aggression, Chamberlain declared that, nevertheless, to continue sanctions when Italy had already won the campaign would be "the very midsummer of madness." The chancellor of the exchequer, away from the House of Commons, jumped into the province of the foreign secretary and delivered himself of a few acid observations on the international situation!

There is no evidence or likelihood that the matter had been discussed at a Cabinet. Chamberlain's greatest admirers have called this exploit "very courageous." Others described it differently. When Baldwin was questioned in the House he was as pale as a ghost, and his face was convulsed with nervousness. Lloyd George had something to say about Chamberlain's unconventional conduct. Just before the end of a classic piece of invective in the House of Commons on June 18th, he said, "The chancellor of the exchequer is heir to the throne and recently he has been trying the crown on to see how it fits. I hope for his own sake that it does not. He has not merely tried the crown on. He has wielded the scepter—which is just the sort of thing that heirs do when there are weak monarchs." Then came a passage where, by quoting an election manifesto, Lloyd George held up Chamberlain as a self-condemned coward.

Though he may have invited this charge, it was false. Right or wrong, he has always had the courage of his convictions. When he became prime minister after Baldwin had successfully seen the new king crowned, that courage led him to do unusual things. He boldly conceived himself as a man with a personal mission in one of the spheres for which he had not been trained—foreign affairs. It must not be inferred that there is any ground for saying that a prime minister should submit slavishly to the Foreign Office and the foreign secretary. His word should be decisive, and he should certainly seek to equip himself with knowledge of the world. But he is unwise if he acts constantly without reference to his foreign secretary and continues to ignore his advice. When he became prime minister Chamberlain was quite unfamiliar with the science of diplomacy and blind to the character of the men he intended to conciliate.

His diagnosis was probably simple and, within certain limits, correct. Germany was a danger but she could perhaps be made amenable to reason, especially the kind of reason he would wield himself. Above all, Italy must be detached from her side. Germany, if isolated, could not hope to win a war and might be expected to abstain from provoking one. In combination with Italy she would be more aggressive and far more formidable.

So the process of conciliating Mussolini was begun. Chamberlain sent him a cordial letter, and it is impossible to believe that Anthony Eden, his foreign secretary, could have been a party to its dispatch. For a year Mussolini had been fomenting and fostering Franco's rebellion. These activities had to be endured and even palliated while the object of Anglo-Italian friendship was pursued. It is difficult to recall any occasion when Chamberlain brought himself to reprove Mussolini for continually breaking the Nonintervention Agreement and pouring in men and munitions to Franco's side. "Friendship with Italy" was a policy that had to endure every strain.

Anthony Eden, who had been the pupil, protégé, and confidant of Sir Austen, found Neville Chamberlain's methods and the principles of his policy contrary to his own convictions. So Eden went in February, 1938. From May, 1937, to March, 1939, men speculated on countless occasions "what Austen would have said" of the various changes that marked our foreign policy. To him, as to Churchill, Germany had been the abiding danger. For nearly two years the policy of appeasement contributed to the strengthening of Germany and to the enfeebling of possible resistance to her.

The death of Austen when Neville was within a few weeks of adding a Chamberlain to the scroll of prime ministers must have seemed a devilish tragedy. But, had Austen lived, would the austerity of his scruples have forced him to try to curb what he must have regarded as his brother's willful disregard of danger? Would he have felt bound to stand with Churchill, with Eden, with Cranborne, and with Duff Cooper? Would his counsel have deflected our policy from the course it actually took? Or would fraternal ties have prevailed and should we have seen Austen holding up his brother's hands in crisis and adversity as he had sometimes succored Stanley Baldwin? We must not ignore the possibility that he would have found Neville's conduct of foreign affairs beyond serious reproach, though such approval would seem contrary to known conviction.

By an incalculable process Chamberlain began to acquire in some quarters a reputation for infallibility. This renown reached its zenith during and after the Sudetenland crisis in the autumn of 1938 and was not greatly diminished till German troops entered Prague—violating Hitler's promise to Chamberlain—in March, 1939. Even then it was replaced in the hearts of many only by compassion for a wise and good man who had been cruelly deceived by a low foreigner.

Eden was succeeded by Lord Halifax, a man equally willing with Chamberlain to assign excellence of motive to difficult characters. This charity of outlook is admirable where purely personal relationships are concerned. Where the safety of the community is at stake it must have a limit. At some moment, to quote Lord Halifax, we must declare, "Halt! Major road ahead."

Chamberlain and Halifax began their task hopefully. They thought that Nazi ambitions could be sated before too much would be lost, and that a rational psychology would follow satiety. They tried to attribute to the Nazi hierarchy the same decent instincts that inspired themselves. Halifax had to learn from experience that Goebbels was made of different stuff from Gandhi. The chief Nazi personalities are not a body of devoted saints. Halifax and Chamberlain had a heartbreaking task as they tried to satisfy these cormorants and appease the implacable.

After the invasion of Bohemia, the Conservative Central Office, whose propaganda is excellent, recapitulated part of the tale of Hitler's fraudulent dealing. Some have regretted that this tune was not sung twelve months earlier. The periodic Conservative publication *Hints for Speakers* is a model of utilitarian propaganda and is available for anyone to purchase. Its facts are usually authentic and it sets an example to other parties whose methods are less tidy and more immoderate. When it was found necessary to remember Hitler's plentiful duplicities the Conservative literature set some of them out in telling array. The Conservative leader must have had in mind what Central Office had at its finger tips. Here were some of the means of testing Hitler's character—facts present in the minds of all with a shred of memory:

After Hitler's early triumph in the Saar in January, 1935, apprehensions about possible German policy were lulled by a period of external quiet. With great cunning the German chancellor let it be concluded that Europe could settle down to calm, however brutal the persecutions he instituted against his enemies at home. On March 7, 1936, Germany reoccupied the demilitarized zone of the Rhineland, which had been established under the Treaty of Locarno, a freely negotiated instrument whose obligations Hitler had reaffirmed. Simultaneously he declared that he had no more territorial demands to make in Europe.

In July, 1936, Hitler recognized Austrian independence under a bilateral agreement between himself and Austria. In 1937 he stated that the period of surprises was over. On March 11, 1938, while Dr. Schuschnigg was bending before the hurricane of German bullying, a German army invaded Austria. Chamberlain, in a written statement which he read to the House of Commons, observed that this act of violence must have "a damaging influence upon general confidence in Europe." On the same day (March 11th) Goering gave an assurance to the Czechoslovak minister in Berlin about the benevolent intentions of Germany toward Czechoslovakia and later expressly renewed the assurance on Hitler's behalf. On March 12th the Czechoslovak minister in Berlin was assured by von Neurath that Germany considered herself bound by the German-Czechoslovak Convention for Arbitration of October, 1925. These assurances were cited by Chamberlain in the House on March 14th. For some reason they are omitted from the catalogue of German treachery in the relevant number of *Hints for Speakers*.

In the course of his celebrated statement on "crisis Wednesday" (September 28, 1938), Chamberlain told the House of Commons that at Berchtesgaden Hitler had repeated to him that the Sudetenland was the last of his territorial ambitions in Europe and that he had no wish to include in his realm people of other races than Germans.

On September 26th in a speech in Berlin Hitler said, "We do not want any Czechs." The Munich agreement provided for the final determination of the frontiers of the new Czechoslovak state by the international commission. Germany occupied Bohemia on the ides of March, 1939.

Two days followed during which some men entertained unnecessary doubts as to what would be Chamberlain's reactions. Then in a speech at Birmingham he showed himself convinced about the Nazi character and converted beyond recall from his former attitude of trustfulness. He had certainly given the Nazi leaders abundant rope. No doubt Chamberlain had supplemented his knowledge of Hitler's record by dipping into *Mein Kampf*. Chamberlain was in the dreadful position of having, till war became inevitable, to treat the Nazis in Germany as though they were as civilized as we are.

Let us trace the course of Chamberlain's efforts to find an honorable alternative to the catastrophe of war. The whole story is contained in just over a single year. It may be begun with a House of Commons occasion—the debate on the resignation of Eden and Cranborne, which occupied two days of parliamentary time. Though this was the most unpleasant crisis he had yet had to face, Chamberlain showed his stamina by delivering three speeches of first-rate importance in these two days.

In the first speech he contended that the peace of Europe must depend on Germany, Italy, France, and ourselves. In the second, delivered at the end of the first day, he explained that he had omitted Russia because she was partly European and partly Asiatic. At the end of the second day he spoke in the vein both of the prime minister of Great Britain and of the leader of a political party well able to bring discomfiture to the Opposition. He is a first-class debater and he cannot always suppress a smile as he sees his blows going home. He is able to make opponents afraid of him. He taunted the Opposition for their faith in "collective security" and then denied that the League as then constituted could afford protection to small weak nations. He publicly declared that, while at the last election he had believed that the League might still afford collective security, he believed it no longer. In this context he called the Labor party "the worst kind of diehards." It seemed as though Eden's departure meant to Chamberlain a welcome occasion for outspokenness.

Now, what Chamberlain did after March, 1939, may not have been solemnized before the high altar at Geneva, but every country on the west and east of Europe which entered the peace front and to whom Chamberlain gave a guarantee was a member state of the League. And fifteen months' experience was enough to make Chamberlain go to a great deal of trouble, when trying to protect the interests of states against violent interference, in his efforts to attract the support of the "partly Asiatic" Russians.

Chamberlain reads Shakespeare for refreshment and enjoys hearing and playing Beethoven. No doubt he is fully familiar with the witches' incantation in *Macbeth* and the unflagging motif that runs through the Fifth Symphony. From the moment of the submergence of Austria till our return under the compulsion of events to the principles of the Covenant the name that recurred again and again in our political anxieties with its burden of toil and trouble was "Czechoslovakia."

But to too many of Chamberlain's followers Czechoslovakia did not mean a free and valiant outpost against the advance of a power whose values and intentions were at strife with all for which Great Britain stood. In their ignorance they regarded her as a patchwork republic whose existing form was an incitement to the more irritable side of Hitler's nature. So she was, in their eyes, a nuisance; not a breakwater against the tide of tyranny, but a powder magazine inconveniently situated in the center of Europe.

As long ago as the Austrian crisis it had become necessary for Chamberlain to declare our policy about the future of Czechoslovakia. On March 24, 1938, he returned to the subject. He began by casting a few darts at the Opposition and quoted the official Labor paper, the *Daily Herald*, in support of his thesis that collective security under the League was no longer possible. Then followed an oft-quoted passage. He declined to guarantee Czechoslovakia. He showed that at the moment he would have nothing to do with automatic obligations. He added these words: "If war broke out it would be unlikely to be confined to those who have assumed legal obligations. . . . This is especially true in the case of two countries like Great Britain and France . . . devoted to the same ideals of democratic liberty and determined to uphold them."

What exactly was in the minds of Chamberlain, Hoare, Simon, and the rest at this moment? Perhaps they imagined that this warning, with its somewhat equivocal context, would be formidable enough to discourage Hitler's designs. We may never know the debates and discussions that attended the composition of Chamberlain's speech. The majority, with Chamberlain's personality dominating the Cabinet room, did not yet deem it desirable or necessary to challenge the Nazis: "Try it on and we fight!" Unfortunately, it proved useless merely to point out that a certain course of action might lead to regrettable consequences.

Most likely the same majority regarded with profound apprehension the possibility of having—as we know, from Duff Cooper's speech of resignation, they described it— "to fight for Czechoslovakia." One man certainly had no doubts about her strategic value; his name is Hitler. One thing he had learnt from Bismarck: "The master of Bohemia is the master of Europe."

Such indignation as had been felt in England against Chamberlain was now directed in a fiercer volume against Hitler. Parliament could no longer remain unsummoned. All was set for the intense scenes of September 28th.

It is absurdly untrue to say, as ingenious gossips have repeated, that when Chamberlain began his long statement he knew the dramatic manner in which his speech would end. He may have imagined that a favorable communication might come through at some moment during the day. But it is a fantastic thing to say that Halifax and he had plotted that the message should be handed to Halifax in the peers' gallery at 4:15 and that it should then be hurriedly passed into Chamberlain's hand as he was speaking.

Just before he ended at 4:22, Chamberlain announced that his personal message to Mussolini had resulted in the Duce's interceding with Hitler and persuading him to agree to postpone mobilization for twenty-four hours. He then conveyed Hitler's message which had just arrived, inviting him to Munich on Thursday morning. "I need not say what my answer will be." The scene that followed has often been described. One member on the government benches yelled, "Thank God for Neville!" "Neville" asked to be released and for the adjournment of the debate. Short speeches of good wishes were uttered by the leaders of the different parties. Mr. William Gal-

lacher, the Communist, was an exception amid the general
thanksgiving. "I protest," he shouted, "against the dis-
memberment of Czechoslovakia." Some members wept
with relief and muttered their thanks to the Almighty.
The House was up before 4:30. Winston Churchill moved
up to the Front Bench. He shook hands with Chamberlain and is alleged to have muttered, "My God, Neville,
you have all the luck!"

This demonstration, I believe, had a tremendous effect
upon Chamberlain. He saw around him the representatives of the British people standing up, waving their
order papers, cheering a great reprieve. He found himself bound to produce peace and produce it quickly. So,
as he was leaving next morning for Munich, he was heard
to observe, "It will be all right this time." Right up to the
publication of the terms of the Munich agreement there
were many members of Parliament who were saying,
"This is Hitler's first setback. He knows if he goes on he
will meet with war and disaster. Chamberlain has at last
shown him the face of resolution. We have been wrong
in our apprehensions and criticisms. After all, the old
man has broken the Rome-Berlin Axis."

Alas for these rosy speculations! If the Munich "settlement" was in some respects less terrible than the Godesberg ultimatum, few persons knew enough about them to
specify the differences; in any case, if they existed, they
did not survive long. Faced now with a joint ultimatum
by France, Britain, Germany, and Italy—"I expect an
answer by midday" was Chamberlain's bidding—the
Czechoslovak Republic bowed down to the earth under
a cruel weight of sorrow. The British prime minister
flew back home. Benes retired into the darkness. At Hes-
ton Airport Chamberlain held up the declaration made

jointly by himself and Hitler. It was a typed document,
signed in an illegible scrawl by the German chancellor
above the admirably clear calligraphy of the British prime
minister. In the left-hand bottom corner Neville Chamberlain had added the date. The characters of the two
men stare out from the paper in their contrasted hand-
writing: Hitler mean, untutored, paranoiac; Chamberlain punctilious, lucid, resolute, honorable.

When he had enjoyed the congratulations of his sovereign in Buckingham Palace and a quasi-royal progress
home to Downing Street, he had to come on to the bal-
cony of No. 10 and "say a few words." Here was a man
thrust through accident and circumstance into the position of a national hero by a section of the populace which
neither knew what was happening nor what it would
mean for them. He was psychologically if not physically
fatigued. He, who had never attracted the limelight, had
been fantastically feted. This is part of what he was heard
to say:

"My good friends, this is the second time in our history
that there has come back from Germany to Downing
Street peace with honor . . . I believe it is peace for our
time . . . I recommend you to go home and sleep
quietly in your beds." To produce this synthetic composition Neville Chamberlain had recourse to Disraeli, to
the Anglican liturgy, and to the late Lord Fisher. Films
were made cobbling together every episode in his mis-
sions. For this exhibition one cinema proprietor expected
a great, though perhaps a transitory, popularity; he had
set up outside his theater a poster: "Chamberlain the
Peacemaker; for one week only."

Historians will insist upon judging Chamberlain by
his foreign policy, and biographers are no doubt already

preparing to swoop like vultures directly he retires. Already the chapter of "appeasement" is ended. The most ardent apologists can hardly claim for it an illustrious success, but it is interesting to see what those apologists found to say—and still say—in defense of Munich. Let their case be set out and answered if it can be.

"There was no alternative to Munich but war." That is pure conjecture. Why did Hitler postpone his own mobilization directly the British Fleet was mobilized? Should a great nation always be pressed into surrender by the threat of war? Did not Munich make inevitable the final collapse of the remnant and so give Hitler far greater strategic advantages for the waging of any future war?

"The people of Britain would never have sanctioned an automatic guarantee of Czechoslovakia's integrity." If he made this statement, Chamberlain underrated his own influence. If the people could condone his mistakes, they would have responded to his leadership. Why did not the guarantees to Poland and the rest arouse a storm of protestation? Democracy will respond to guidance and leadership. A wholly united nation with its eyes wide open has followed Chamberlain into a war which Britain undertook to fulfill her automatic guarantee to Poland.

"The defenses of Great Britain were not in a fit condition at the moment of Munich." Chamberlain has never himself said this—he only admitted the existence of "certain gaps in our defenses"—but it was the trump card of his apologists. They were really uttering the most serious condemnation. It is no use their trying to shift the blame onto the shoulders of Baldwin or MacDonald. For seven years, up to Munich, Chamberlain was first or second minister. A mandate for rearmament had been obtained at the last election in 1935. In three years it had not been

used well enough to give us a formidable proficiency!
Today we are certainly far stronger than in September,
1938. It is the business of all governments to see that their
country always possesses adequate armed strength, and
how long will it take Britain to make up for the loss of
the heights of Bohemia and of the stout valor of the
Czechoslovak Army—to say nothing of the mighty arsenal
at Pilsen?

The controversy over Munich will never disappear.
What matters most is that, whatever may have been right
at Munich in September, Chamberlain has given Britain
the chance to right the great and undeniable wrong the
Czechs suffered in March.

Mr. Chamberlain may have intended putting the
copingstone on his edifice of appeasement by legalizing
the entry of the Nazis into Africa. However, a new shadow
soon darkened the European garden when Hitler began
his Jewish pogrom in November. "Does the prime minister," he was asked in the House of Commons, amid
deafening cheers, "think that Germany is fit for colonial
possessions?"

When the whole Munich fabric collapsed in ruins in
March, Chamberlain looked shocked and surprised. I
think his appearance was a sincere indication of the bitter
disappointment that invaded him; he had genuinely believed that Hitler would keep his word. From that moment he was a gentler being. It is true that he laid about
him with great force two days later at Birmingham when
he had measured the public reaction. From now on he
showed himself fully aware of the dangers threatening
the British Commonwealth.

For months after Munich he seemed easily provoked by
the normal processes of Opposition. Once he began a

reply to a supplementary question by the unfortunate statement, "I am not here to be cross-examined about—" A shout went up, a shout with perhaps some justification, for is it not in order that he may be directly answerable to the public's representatives that the prime minister receives a thousand dollars a week? He saw his mistake, smiled, and righted himself.

Poor Mr. Ramsay MacDonald, standing at the dispatch box in the midst of some curvilinear sentence devoid of construction, sense, and punctuation, seemed sometimes to be saying to himself as he paused, "By Jove, I'm prime minister! What a sight for tired eyes!" This conceit was laughable, but harmless. Neville Chamberlain had not conceit, but supreme self-confidence. What was in *his* mind might be, "I'm headmaster and, by heaven, I will be both master and head."

He was able to assess the talents of his colleagues, to all of whom he was undeniably superior. He used to undertake all the major tasks of speaking himself, a habit not always appreciated by other ministers. He has always been able to appeal to the massive loyalty of the great majority of his supporters. "I may have my faults but this is not one of them." Cheering would cover up any deficiency.

One great advantage about his personality is that he enjoys the confidence of all the business community, who have preferred short-range peace to present risks with the possibility of long-term security. They may have been as blind to the vast but inevitable risks associated with the enormous area to whose freedom Chamberlain was obliged to pledge British treasure and British blood as they were to the fatal consequences of allowing state after state to fall under Nazi dominion.

But perhaps it is as well that they were too loyal to criticize when he had to do the one thing that might salvage freedom. Criticism of their hero used to be laughed away by the undemocratic plea, "He must know better than any of us." Today that remark is not an empty one. Neville Chamberlain has learned, he is a man of stubborn determination, and if, during the time that remains to him, he presses on with the war as loyally as he struggled to maintain peace, posterity will thank him for clearing Europe of the Terror.

Some have called him a Fascist. It is a ludicrous charge. Freedom of opinion is as absolute with him as prime minister as it has ever been. And after months of grim self-restraint his real feelings on Nazi repression have shown themselves. His actions entitle him to the noblest motto: "Let life perish rather than liberty."

The quaint theory about Chamberlain's leaning toward dictatorship has perhaps been encouraged by the contrast he made with his two predecessors, Stanley Baldwin and Ramsay MacDonald, who alternated as prime minister for fourteen years before his own elevation. MacDonald was the despair of all who demand and admire clarity; when he was criticized he would allow himself to be wounded and would embark on the most elaborate self-justification. He would fret and fulminate. Asquith, when making the speech which killed the first Labor administration and incidentally preceded his own electoral fall, referred to MacDonald's "sacrosanct supersensitiveness." Often the loudness of his voice alone gave MacDonald's supporters the signal for applause. At the same time he liked to make contacts with others who admired him and were not rivals. He had a certain charm of manner which often conciliated many whom his furious public obscurities had exasperated.

Baldwin seemed bent on giving the world the notion that he was an easygoing, fallible human being. It was an astute and misleading impression. His premiership was not what it appeared to be—the apotheosis of the ordinary man. He had great depths of worldly wisdom which enabled him to select subordinates, disarm opposition, and excite loyalty. No one has ever contrived more thoroughly or more naturally to sink to the level of his companions. He may have reduced the habit of playing for time to a fine art, but he was neither blind nor slow-witted. Beneath the plain and massive exterior was a mind of subtlety and discernment.

Yet, just because Baldwin seemed so commonplace he could command a loyalty that sustained him, a Tory leader, as he marched over thin ice and through the dangerous valleys of radicalism. Here we can detect part of the secret force that enabled him, in spite of a general strike, to cool class hatreds to a point where they ceased to be perilous, to place India on the highroad to responsible government, and to carry this monarchist country safely through the dreadful crisis of the abdication. At such moments Stanley Baldwin could stand out as the unchallenged epitome of the entire nation.

Neville Chamberlain's strength is different. No critic has ever called his statements obscure or his habits easygoing. He seems to hate all that is flowery, negligent, or rhetorical. That may be one of the reasons why he is a first-class broadcaster. Many prominent public figures have been failures at the microphone. They forget that they are neither addressing a public meeting nor coruscating in debate. Their task is to speak naturally and

directly to one or two individuals sitting at their fireside
with a wireless set in the corner of a private room. And
by some happy accident Neville Chamberlain possesses
the right technique. At the microphone he does not lecture, he does not hector, he *talks*. Consequently, he
broadcasts better than he speaks or debates, though his
dialectical powers are of a high order.

Often a first-class statement of policy in the House of
Commons has fallen from his lips in tones so subdued as
barely to reach the press gallery. From his speeches every
superfluous word has been ruthlessly sweated out. His case
is clear to himself; he expects it to be clear to his audience.
If they do not take it in or if they fail to agree, he is
impatient of their obtuseness. Once at a meeting he
humorously exaggerated this characteristic: "I do not
object to criticism provided I have my own way."

This feature has been seized by others and distorted to
a monstrous size. At the worst, it is an amiable weakness;
at best, it is evidence of an admirable determination
which is too rare in an age when hesitations paralyze the
good intentions. Tireless, and strong of will, Neville
Chamberlain has striven to keep the community in the
ways of peace and prosperity. Hitler has thwarted him.
But we know well enough to which man history will
attribute uprightness of purpose and Christian meekness
of spirit.

Among English politicians, Neville Chamberlain has
had the completest opportunity of weighing the character
and analyzing the personality of the German dictator. He
detests the perfidy that has wrecked the peace of Europe.
Not only has Hitler lied to the Austrians, the Czechs,
and the Poles; he has also deceived and insulted the

British prime minister. Chamberlain will never forgive Hitler unless and until he is rendered harmless.

Mr. Chamberlain intensely desired "peace for our time," but when it could have been bought only at the cost of every shred of British honor he did not shrink from the dark path of duty. Critics tomorrow may point to certain of his actions and say, "This or that was a cardinal mistake. After that particular point war with Germany or surrender to her demands became for Britain the inevitable dilemma," and so on. They may contend that Hitler, after meeting Chamberlain, was disastrously convinced that Britain would never stand in his path until he was so powerful that he could blackmail her to his heart's content.

The critics may be right or they may be wrong. But these and kindred comments are today irrelevant. What matters is that at the end Chamberlain has sounded the doom of Nazidom. No way is now open to us save this great and dangerous crusade. Chamberlain has led us into it: for that we are grateful—and also compassionate.

Why is sorrowful sympathy appropriate? Read these words spoken in the British House of Commons in almost a whisper by a man pale with toil and grief. A few minutes before, the "Raiders Passed" signal had sounded after our first air raid alarm. The time was noon of Sunday, September 3rd:

"This is a sad day for all of us, and to none is it sadder than to me. Everything that I have worked for, everything that I have hoped for, everything that I have believed in during my public life, has crashed into ruins. There is only one thing left for me to do; that is, to devote what strength and powers I have to forwarding the victory of the cause for which we have to sacrifice so much. I cannot

tell what part I may be allowed to play myself; I trust I
may live to see the day when Hitlerism has been destroyed
and a liberated Europe has been re-established."

So spoke Neville Chamberlain, and never had he
spoken less like a party leader and more like a representative of the British people. These words, the end of his
speech to the House of Commons, announcing the German failure to reply to the British ultimatum, followed,
at an interval of just over sixteen hours, a speech which
had left the House and the public in a state of bewilderment. It now appears that the prime minister had had to
keep as close touch as possible with our French allies.
They needed a few more hours. He had to temporize.

Late that Saturday night members of the Cabinet had
struggled to No. 10 Downing Street through darkened
streets swept by rain and wind, illuminated now and then
by flashes of lightning and echoing with the crackles of
ominous thunder. They took their decision to dispatch
an ultimatum on Sunday morning. Whatever our French
allies might do, Britain was pledged and the House of
Commons showed on Saturday evening that Britain's
pledge to aid Poland must be honored without further
delay.

Go back yet another twenty-four hours and the real
Chamberlain can be heard again—a man bitterly disap-
pointed at the failure of his efforts to restrain Hitler,
overburdened by a heavy and mounting weight of toil,
and nauseated by the savage duplicities of the Nazis. Thus
he had spoken in Parliament on Friday, September 1st:

"It now only remains for us to set our teeth and to
enter upon this struggle, which we ourselves earnestly
endeavored to avoid, with determination to see it through
to the end. We shall enter it with a clear conscience, with

the support of the Dominions and the British Empire, and the moral approval of the greater part of the world. We have no quarrel with the German people, except that they allow themselves to be governed by a Nazi government. As long as that government exists and pursues the methods it has so persistently followed during the last two years there will be no peace in Europe. We shall merely pass from one crisis to another, and see one country after another attacked by methods which have now become familiar to us in their sickening technique. We are resolved that these methods must come to an end. If out of the struggle we again establish in the world the rules of good faith and the renunciation of force, why, then even the sacrifices that will be entailed upon us will find their fullest justification."

Tomorrow the historian may be arguing that, after his successes at Munich and Prague, Hitler always believed that Chamberlain would recoil from throwing the weight of Britain into the scales on the side of freedom. But if he reads the correspondence which passed between the British and German governments, August 22 to 31, 1939, he will have to concede that over the Polish crisis Chamberlain cannot be reproached with the faintest shadow of obscurity. If Hitler was capable of being convinced he must have known by the end of August that Britain was coming into the war he had planned, and against Germany.

Before Britain steps into the sunlight of victory she may have to endure many days of disappointment, darkness, and despair. Now and then the voice of pacifist defeatism may be heard. If some of our friends are at first overwhelmed, we may be sure that here and there the plea will be audible: "Why go on fighting? We can't protect our friends. Let us make a separate peace without further bloodshed."

To this sort of pleading we may be sure Neville Chamberlain, so long as he is prime minister, will be studiously and deliberately deaf. Nobody knows better than he what an abominable and treacherous thing we are fighting. He has touched and seen the enemy; he has felt the devil that possesses him. He has lived through the anxieties, hopes, and disappointments of a long struggle to persuade Hitler to behave with a little human decency. The first part of his enterprise has failed, so the battle has had to be joined. No tolerable peace can come till Hitler's power is destroyed. Not from Chamberlain, we may be sure, will come any flinching or wavering in the grim labor of the overthrowing of those "evil things that we are fighting against—brute force, bad faith, injustice, oppression, and persecution."

CHAPTER III

WINSTON CHURCHILL

The Admirable Crichton

WHEN in England you speak of "Winston" nobody
is in any doubt who is intended. You are referring
to the Right Honorable Winston Leonard Spencer
Churchill, Companion of Honor, member of Parliament,
—the man who became first lord of the admiralty in the
War Cabinet of nine formed immediately upon the beginning of the Second German War on September 3, 1939.
But if you mention "Winston Churchill" in the United
States your companion, unless he is very young, might
guess that you mean the American author of historical
novels who was particularly well known earlier in this
century.

There is a story, for the authenticity of which I do not
vouch, that when the English edition found his fame
spreading beyond the shores of Britain and the boundaries
of Europe he wrote to his namesake in the United States.
He suggested that, as there were two celebrated figures
bearing the same name, it might obviate confusion if one
of them would make some adjustment in the name by
which he was known to the world. The story ends with
the reply of the American: he was not aware of the
existence of more than one famous Winston Churchill.

I include this anecdote at this stage only because of its
rarity. It is one of the very few stories about the English

Winston Churchill in which he comes off second best. But he would himself enjoy it, as his alleged vanquisher belongs to a nation with whom he has long had the closest ties. Winston Churchill owes his mother to America. He and his son Randolph have visited America, have toured America, and have lectured in America. To his unfamiliarity with American traffic regulations he owes a recent accident. It left a scar on his face which will last for the remainder of his life.

Better than many other Englishmen, Winston Churchill has measured the decisive contribution made by the United States to the course of the First German War. No belittler of the American effort need argue that, with a population three times as great as that of Great Britain, the United States lost in killed not more than a twenty-fifth of the total British dead. Apart from the virile intervention of the American armies on the western front and their gallant participation in the offensives of the final summer, the German High Command were progressively depressed by the knowledge that fresh troops were monthly pouring across the Atlantic by the hundred thousand. After their terrible spring offensive had petered out, the Germans knew they were doomed to defeat.

Of this incalculable service to the Allied cause Winston Churchill, himself once a soldier, has always been fully and gratefully conscious. He is too intelligent a man to imagine that the islands on the northwest of the European mainland can ever divorce themselves from the affairs of the Continent. But he rightly reposes the highest hopes for the survival of civilization in the friendship of the English-speaking peoples.

Today his significance is international. Even the Nazis, who are astonishingly inaccurate about domestic affairs

in Great Britain, have been thoroughly aware of Churchill's stature as an adversary. Their explanation that Mr.
Churchill sank the *Athenia* in order to bring in the
United States on the side of France and Great Britain
was only the first of many violent attacks which showed
that they rated him as their most dangerous foe.

What are the elements of heredity and environment
which have made Winston Churchill the most feared of
foes, the most formidable of controversialists, and at last
the most universally admired individual in English public life? He never forgets, nor should his critics allow
themselves to forget, that he is the grandson of a duke and
a direct descendant of Marlborough, probably the greatest soldier in the history of Britain.

Biology decrees that Winston shall always be fighting;
his nature needs victory as keenly as it loves battle. It has
often been said that he belongs to the harder-hitting
Edwardian school of politicians. He was born in 1874, but
even if his birth had been postponed for thirty years
Winston Churchill would have always found opponents
to hit and foes to wound.

His father, Lord Randolph Churchill, lived only forty-
five years, but twenty of them were devoted to a political
career of fearless and aggressive activity. By the time he
was thirty-seven Lord Randolph had been secretary of
state for India, chancellor of the exchequer, and leader of
the House of Commons.

Lord Randolph had a deep influence upon Winston,
though at the father's death the son was but twenty. He
took his politics from his father almost without question.
They were a type of politics peculiar to Britain. They
are defined as "Tory Democracy"; they constitute a belief
that the masses of working people can be rightly led to

regard themselves as the chief defenders of the institutions by which their political liberties and economic progress have been secured. When this inspiration is borne in mind, the career of Winston Churchill with its apparent inconsistencies and unexpectedly generous impulses is far easier to understand.

Two schools are most favored by the more fortunate classes of English people—Eton and Harrow. Winston was sent to Harrow, and then on to Sandhurst, the English West Point. Within five years of his being commissioned he had fought in five campaigns. He was present at the Battle of Khartoum under Kitchener. But the most exciting interlude of this adventurous period was his part in the South African War. He was traveling on an armored train which the Boers derailed. Since it was necessary to keep climbing in and out of the cab of the engine. Churchill found that his pistol encumbered him and laid it aside. When the Boers opened fire on the derailed train, Churchill tried to get away along the railway line.

He became isolated from his companions, and some minutes later a Boer officer galloped up and ordered Churchill to surrender. Churchill had left his only weapon behind, so, after looking sorrowfully up and down the line and seeing that no help was in sight, he put up his hands.

The name of his captor was Botha, who afterward became commander in chief of the Boers. After the eventual British victory in the war and the granting of home rule to South Africa by the Liberal government in London—of which Churchill was a member—this same Botha became prime minister of the Union of South Africa. And he was mainly instrumental in quelling the South African rebellion which broke out in 1914 at the beginning of the

First German War. Thus accident—or Providence—preserved both Churchill and Botha for vital service to the British Commonwealth of Nations.

But Churchill was not to remain a prisoner. Within four weeks he had escaped. His exploits, his antecedents, and his lately discovered powers of speech had made him famous. A general election was held in 1900—popularly known as "The Khaki Election." Winston was nominated as a Conservative and elected to Parliament, at the age of twenty-five.

In appearance, this soldier turned statesman is short and thickset. He seems dedicated by destiny to combat. His battles may be physical or intellectual. He takes great strides over the floor of the House of Commons or along the lobbies. As he marches forward he looks full of purpose. His round face is normally fixed in stern lines. But his is no elderly severity. He still looks as though the months he spent in his cradle were a specially significant part of his career.

A Tory woman, fulminating before the First German War against what she imagined were his satanic works, raged, "The baby face of that traitor Winston Churchill drives me mad." If she had seen him in the flesh instead of on the pages of the illustrated press she might not have made such an attack. In all probability she would have been impressed by his resolute appearance or melted by his attractive grin. Nor need she have worried about the safety of England's honor in his charge. Winston Churchill has for long been able to give many of his fellow citizens lessons in patriotism.

Twenty years ago when I first heard him speak I began by thinking he was half-witted. A moment later I was imagining that he had dined too well. I ended by utter capitulation. At first he halted and stammered; he could not cope properly with a soft "s." I heard, instead, an odd sound which the radio has more recently sent a score of times across the Atlantic to American listeners.

To take a fantastic parallel from *Alice in Wonderland*, when I heard him for the first time, it seemed for a moment that one of Lewis Carroll's "mome raths" had come to life; here was one outgribing and outgribing publicly. Humpty Dumpty had to explain that outgribing was "something between bellowing and whistling with a kind of sneeze in the middle . . . when you've once heard it, you'll be *quite* content." Churchill produces the opposite effect. Once heard he makes you want more; he always seems to sit down too soon. He is too big a man to be sensitive about this unique crackling sound. When, as an escaped prisoner of war, he was wanted by the Boers, they advertised this disability as a means of identification.

He is conscious of his own size and knows how to whet the public interest in himself. He warms his audience—as Mr. Lloyd George does also—by constantly inviting them to laugh with him at Winston Churchill. "One of the most moderate remarks I have ever been privileged to make" . . . "I support the prime minister; I hope that by so doing I shall do him no harm." Once he was rebuking Lord Snowden, the former Socialist chancellor of the exchequer, for senile bitterness: "I say to myself, 'Winston, as you ripen, you must mellow.'"

It is impossible to forget his face and figure. On his return to the Admiralty in September, 1939, Churchill was given a pass which would enable him to go in and out of these headquarters of the navy at any hour of the day or night without challenge. He glanced at the ticket, then tore it up and threw it aside. "My face," he said, "is my fortune." That is the measure of his respect for red tape.

In a stubborn mood Churchill suggests a bulldog. A puckish temper animates him and in a flash he has turned into the most brilliant of clowns. The last thing that could truthfully be said about him is that he is an anachronism. He is fully alive to all international and domestic problems of the day, and is eager to describe and resolve them by an original felicity of phrase. Forty years ago he arrived at two philosophies: radicalism and imperialism. On this basis his dizziest somersaults become rational and almost inevitable.

Winston Churchill has twice changed his party. He began his political life as a Conservative, but at the beginning of the twentieth century the Conservative ascendancy in British politics was fated rapidly to dwindle. By the time that he had been in Parliament for four years Joseph Chamberlain was splitting the Conservative party by his campaign for tariffs. Churchill was intellectually a freetrader. In 1904 he joined the Liberals, and with them he remained for nearly twenty years. His return at the Liberal "landslide" of 1906 became a foregone conclusion.

Churchill's critics have called this transfiguration "political inconsistency number one." But from the other point of view he was right in joining and helping to lead a widespread revulsion against a policy which a great majority of the public thought to be stupid and immoral. If so many of the public were right, it is hard to see how the youthful Churchill can have been wrong. Few men have been more openly ambitious. But why should not desire and duty coincide?

Until recent years when a member of the Commons

was elevated to the Cabinet he had to seek re-election by his constituents. When Asquith became prime minister in 1908 he made Churchill president of the Board of Trade. Churchill was defeated at the by-election, for by that time the tide of Liberal triumph was beginning to ebb.

He had been a member for Manchester since 1906. Observe how unnecessary it is in English politics for a locality to be represented in Parliament by a "local man." Within *seven minutes* of his defeat at Manchester, Churchill was handed a telegram conveying the unanimous invitation of the Liberal Association in the Scottish city of Dundee, where a vacancy had just occurred, to become their candidate.

For Dundee he sat till 1922, and was then defeated by an Independent candidate whose main plank was prohibition! This gentleman had stood for election in Dundee on six occasions. The first time he polled 300 votes; by the time he defeated Churchill, fifteen years later, he had increased his poll to 35,000. Churchill's opponent represented a revolt against the appalling drunkenness which stained Dundee and gave it a uniquely evil reputation in the United Kingdom. He was a Christian Socialist cast up from the seething masses of poverty-stricken citizens. He called upon God to assist him and, when he was finally returned at the head of the poll, moved the customary vote of thanks, not to the returning officer, but to the Almighty.

Between the ages of thirty-four and forty-eight Winston was at the height of his wonderful energies. Into this period he had crammed the maximum of service and enterprise. As first lord of the admiralty he prepared the navy for the First German War. In 1914 he had ready an armada of vast size and incomparable fighting power.

It is said that his conception of the Dardanelles enterprise was masterly but that he was betrayed by others in its execution. The current chatter when we were losing men by the thousands on the arid slopes of Gallipoli was, "It is the fault of that fellow Churchill: he was after something spectacular." Whether this kind of talk was right or wrong, Churchill fell under a cloud from which his closest friends could not rescue him. He resigned from the government and went at once to the front to serve with the Grenadier Guards. There he learned at first hand the meaning of a German bombardment. By 1917 he was back in office as minister of munitions.

The Armistice of November 11, 1918—all it meant, all it ended, all it promised—challenged Churchill's sense of history and sense of justice. The imperialist in him looked out upon the spectacle of Britain victorious. But the whole of pleasure does not consist for him in flags, pageantry, and martial music. He sent shiploads of food to starving Germany and always shied at the astronomic reparations proposed against the vanquished. He loathed war profiteering and the meanness behind it. There is evidence that he personally would have agreed to a levy on capital. While he may have been excited by battle and by finding language to match those great events, he knew and felt the millions of tragedies behind the din, the shouting, and the drama. Churchill may exult in emergency, but he does not lack imagination.

He was attracted by the great purpose of the League of Nations. To him the League has always been "a great and august institution." But he saw from its birth that its value would be lost if it had not the means of enforcing its decisions. The Rule of Law needed to be sustained by power. In *The Aftermath* Churchill dreams about the might-have-been. A new mechanical force contemptuous of frontiers had developed miraculously under the pressure of hostilities. Why should not the air forces be pledged to the service of the League of Nations? Failure to appreciate and analyze these convictions has led Churchill's critics to charge him with "instability."

During the years immediately after the war his career was an example of the vagaries of democracy. By a crushing majority Dundee rejected Churchill at the election of 1922, when he stood as a Liberal adherent of Mr. Lloyd George. Next year Churchill fared no better as a plain Liberal at West Leicester.

In February, 1924, the Abbey Division of Westminster fell vacant through the death of the sitting member. Churchill stood this time as an Independent. The official Conservative, in a total poll of nearly 23,000, defeated him by 43 miserable votes. Winston may well have thought this result the crowning fatuity of politics.

However, he had learned to rise quickly to the surface. He found that the greatest peril to the realm lay in the continuance of a Labor administration which leaned dangerously toward an understanding with the "footpads of Moscow." At the general election of December, 1924, he was returned to Parliament with a handsome majority as a "Constitutionalist." He asked his electors which they preferred—the red flag or the Union Jack? His sense of humor sometimes allows him to look back with amusement at the label he bore and the things he said. In a few days he was back within the Conservative fold which he had been attacking for twenty years.

Baldwin, the prime minister, was at the head of a huge

majority. One of the sinecure offices in the British government, to which men can be appointed when they are needed as counselors rather than administrators, is "Chancellor of the Duchy of Lancaster"—a high-sounding title which today carries little meaning. Baldwin invited Churchill to No. 10 Downing Street. An amusing, if doubtful, story is told of their meeting: Baldwin, intending to put Churchill in charge of the "Duchy of Lancaster," said, as soon as he entered the room, "Winston, will you be chancellor?" "Yes," said Churchill without a moment's hesitation. He strode out of No. 10 and said to the expectant journalists gathered outside, "I have accepted the office of chancellor of the exchequer!"

As chancellor of the exchequer, Winston insisted on Britain's returning to the gold standard. By artificially raising the value of the pound sterling, this measure inevitably hit Britain's vital export trade. Against this disadvantage the claim was that the pound could now "look the dollar in the face."

Certainly this action caused admiration in the United States. I was in America at the time and a friend sent me a caustic pamphlet by the well-known economist John Maynard Keynes, called this time not *The Economic Consequences of the Peace*, but *The Economic Consequences of Mr. Churchill*. It predicted unemployment and depression. Both predictions were later thoroughly realized, although the pound remained on gold for only half a dozen years. It slid off again at the time of the financial crisis in 1931.

The years from 1924 to 1929 were rather sterile in Churchill's career except for the general strike of 1926. To him this convulsion seemed political blackmail and an anarchist conspiracy. He ran an emergency newspaper, the *British Gazette*, and showed such a pugnacious attitude that people thanked heaven he did not have the supreme responsibility.

Now was the moment for Churchill's most irritating foible to show itself. There was only one man of his caliber in the government—the Earl of Birkenhead, in charge of the India Office. When Churchill looked at the majority of his colleagues he felt he was being required to suffer fools gladly. So he consumed far more of the Cabinet's time and attention than was reasonable. They may have been entertained by his enchanting monologues, but their suspicions were reinforced by his overbearing manner. In their eyes he became the supreme egotist. Winston Churchill began to be his own enemy.

His imperialism matched his arrogance of behavior. But he joyously sustained much of the burden of opposition. He flung himself into the task of hampering his special adversary in the Labor ranks, Chancellor of the Exchequer Philip Snowden. But he did not spare Ramsay MacDonald; the prime minister with his woolly periods and wordy sentimentalities was a perfect target for Churchill shafts. Here is how, on January 28, 1931, he introduced what has perhaps become his most famous gibe:

"I spoke the other day, after he had been defeated in an important division, about his [MacDonald's] wonderful skill in falling without hurting himself. He falls, but up he comes again, smiling, a little disheveled, but still smiling. . . . I remember, when I was a child, being taken to the celebrated Barnum's Circus, which contained an exhibition of freaks and monstrosities, but the exhibit on the program which I most desired to see was the one described as the Boneless Wonder. My parents judged that spectacle would be too revolting and demoralizing for my youthful eyes, and I have waited fifty years to see the Boneless Wonder!"

When MacDonald and Baldwin formed the National administration, Churchill did not get an office; but he quickly caught the ear of the new House of Commons.

On the second day of the debate on the Address he was cracking jokes in the grand manner. After explaining that he was in no way bound to the Baldwin-MacDonald-Samuel triumvirate he said, "However, I am glad to be able to announce to the House that, if I may without disrespect borrow a phrase from the Gracious Speech: 'My relations with foreign powers continue to be friendly.'" Before he sat down he added in a serious passage, "I do not envy them their offices, but I do envy them their opportunities."

He turned to tease the elderly Mr. George Lansbury, sitting like a faithful and bewildered sheepdog as the leader of the tiny Socialist Opposition. As first commissioner of works, Lansbury had introduced bathing facilities into the pool called the Serpentine in the middle of Hyde Park. The scheme had been described as "Lansbury's Lido." "He has," said Churchill of Lansbury, "with perfect sincerity, and with many agreeable turns of phrase and fancy, held up to us always that dim Utopia, which would reduce our civilization to one vast national soup kitchen, surrounded by innumerable municipal bathing pools." George Lansbury got his own back. Once when Churchill had made himself the mouthpiece of a small but noisy faction, Lansbury said, "He usurps a position in this House as if he had a right to walk in, make his speech, walk out, and leave the whole place as if God

Almighty had spoken! . . . He never listens to any other man's speech but his own."

When I begin reading a speech by Winston Churchill I am as arrested as by any well-spun yarn of adventure or espionage. There is a serious temptation to load this chapter with quotations from his speeches, but I must deny myself and my readers a surfeit of that pleasure. They can be read elsewhere by themselves and in their entirety. All I can do is to promise that their English is so fresh and so masterly that attention will not flag. They are more than splendid rhetoric; they are great literature. And they are so witty that, though some of them were delivered years ago, they will cause the most solemn and unsympathetic student to chuckle as he reads.

But a great deal is lost when they are read and not heard. Every argument is pointed by a natural correctitude of gesture. Churchill's features follow and illustrate the words he utters. His voice arrests and excites. And there is the added stimulus of spontaneous debate. His extemporaneous retorts to his opponents are woven with the most exemplary skill into the texture that he has already fashioned.

Churchill does not believe in the possibility of over-preparation. The main outline of his speeches is typed out sentence by sentence. Even the asides, and the minor parentheses, are in the manuscript. Often he seems to forget his notes altogether, but the course of the flight has been set. He will pursue it resolutely, never losing the course in spite of digressions to adorn a point or deflate an adversary. One of his habits is to test in advance and in private some of his phrases upon two or three listeners. But when the moment arrives and the speech is delivered to a packed, expectant and attentive House of Commons, the speaker's lips are smacked as though the morsel is being savored for the first time. Great art is there, but it is elaborately concealed. And the man who most enjoys Churchill's speeches is Winston himself.

He exhibits a variety of moods in turn—satire, attack, warning, tenderness, sentiment. And his private behavior is equally mercurial. Nobody can give a more courtly, a more amiable, greeting or pay a more graceful compliment. Nobody, when sulkiness descends upon him, can give a more faithful imitation of a bear with a sore head. He is the center of the universe. When he was out of office it was only with impatience that he could bother to listen to others as they spoke or conversed. If it was necessary for him to stay and listen to important speeches by others in authority he would fidget about on the central seat that he always occupied. He would gossip away in a series of half-audible grunts. His jokes might be so irreverent as to threaten a neighbor with convulsions. But he is so attractive a being that these habits were condoned.

Here is an instance of his roguish irreverence. After the Munich agreement of 1938, Neville Chamberlain, Birmingham-bred prime minister, enjoyed in some short-sighted circles a tremendous reputation as a great Architect of Peace. A debate was in progress on the grievous disorders between Arabs and Jews in Palestine. Malcolm MacDonald, secretary of state for the colonies, was speaking, and said that he could never forget that these violent disturbances were rife near the birthplace of the "Prince of Peace." Winston Churchill whispered loudly to his neighbor, "I never knew before that Neville was born in Bethlehem!"

His most grievous experience in recent years was the

pain he underwent at the abdication of Edward VIII at the end of 1936. If he really entertained hopes of starting a "King's party," his judgment was abysmally at fault. But with Churchill it may not have been a question of judgment in the sense of taking the popular line. There arose during this funereal episode a crop of stories about Winston trying to persuade the king to retain the crown and favor a faction. I do not accept them. When with tears streaming down his cheeks he begged Mr. Baldwin repeatedly not to do anything "irrevocable," I believe he was animated by an affection and loyalty for his young sovereign that deserved the high title of love. He had known him intimately and had assisted at his progress for most of his princely career.

For a monarch endowed with King Edward's gifts, Churchill felt, there must surely be abundant latitude allowed by a grateful people. He may not have been wrong in a general sense, but this time he misjudged the situation. In the eyes of the British people Edward VIII was doing the one unforgivable thing. He was degrading the monarchy. They would have sustained him with fresh pillars of loyalty if, at the last, he had forgone his desire. But Edward chose not to make the sacrifice, nor did he want the chivalrous allegiance of his old counselor. The man who suffered the greatest injury and the bitterest pain may well have been Winston Churchill.

Yet even this horrid event, culminating in his own utter confusion and distress and involving the citadel of the Constitution, is secondary to the series of warnings which he has uttered over the past five or six years. The British public, with the shadow of war lengthening across the island, forgot his stumblings and provocations, and paid tardy tribute to his vision. In the matter of German rearmament and the real menace of the Nazi dictatorship his voice and his judgment have never faltered. He was first publicly to define the dimensions of the armaments Hitler was building. The public were skeptical. Baldwin denied his figures and later withdrew his denial. But Baldwin was so reliable and Churchill so unstable that Baldwin remained the object of public esteem.

At the outbreak of Hitler's war, it was ten years since Churchill had last held an office of profit under the crown. He filled that interval with political activity. And he was able to enlarge his contributions to the treasury of English literature. With such a background and such a record of service, how did so long a divorce from power and executive authority affect him? He is the most human being alive. If he had not found irksome his exile from authority he would be less than human. Those ten years brought him to the considerable age of sixty-five. In the summer of 1939 the whole political world was asking, Was this the drama's end, or was there yet to be unfolded a more tremendous act?

Since the end of the First German War he had held the offices of secretary of state for war and air, secretary of state for the colonies, and chancellor of the exchequer. He is not a lawyer, so the great office of lord chancellor has never been open to him. The lord chancellor is head of the judiciary and has the task of presiding over the House of Lords. There are in particular three offices which have never been galvanized by his direction. He has not been asked to co-ordinate defense. He has never presided over the Foreign Office. He has not been prime minister. In theory, of course, he could at any moment have resumed any of the offices he held in former days. What stopped him? There were three obstacles: the mistrust and the jealousy of his critics, and his own uncompromising self-sufficiency.

When the fascinating game of Cabinet building is being played and Churchill is mentioned as a possible prime minister, one of the players will invariably say, "Winston lacks one thing—judgment." Having uttered this pontifical condemnation he will sit back and hope that the candidate will be ruled out. That is certainly a serious charge. And it is difficult to rebut because the quality which Mr. Churchill is said to lack baffles precise definition. Two very different things may be implied: either, on the one hand, that he is incapable of reading the popular mind and interpreting the public's transitory fancy, and so fails to do the expedient thing, or else, on the other hand, that, given a set of circumstances, he can seldom if ever make the wise and right decision. The second failing would be the greatest of defects: the first disability might elevate him to the highest rank of statesmanship! Only a half-wit would contend that the people always know what is best for them. But let us assume that the second sense is intended. Will he do the wise thing in a difficult situation?

In the course of an incomparably full official life, Churchill has had to make a thousand decisions of greater or less importance, many of them secret and unrecorded. Every minister of Cabinet rank has a like responsibility. Churchill's task has been multiplied many times in excess of the normal.

As to his powers of vision when not in office, Churchill was never taken in by the dreadfully successful pro-German propaganda that flooded Great Britain. Since the German militarization of the Rhineland in 1936, with one partial setback, Churchill's reputation for clear-sightedness has been rising. The one reverse was the occasion of the Munich agreement when most of the nation suspended their powers of judgment to acclaim what Chamberlain ventured to call "peace with honor." But enough people were awake to the improbability of Hitler's character having undergone a magic change through contact with Mr. Chamberlain to give Churchill a hearing. A politician rarely collects the credit for being right, but in a few short months he and those who agreed with him were bitterly vindicated.

For two reasons I must risk my readers' irritation by giving a few quotations from his speeches. They are magnificent English. Their prophetic power now seems as inevitable as the hammer blows of fate. In November, 1936, Churchill repeated in the House his warning about our unpreparedness: "The government go on in strange paradox, decided only to be undecided, resolved to be irresolute, adamant for drift, solid for fluidity, all-powerful to be impotent. So we go on preparing more months and years—precious, perhaps vital, to the greatness of Britain—for the locusts to eat. They will say to me, 'A minister of supply is not necessary, for all is going well.' I deny it." It was nearly two years after the delivery of that speech that the agreement of Munich was being excused on the ground of our relative weakness. After a further six months, Mr. Chamberlain made a minister of supply out of a distinguished linguist. It was at the end of the debate from which I have just quoted that Mr. Baldwin explained that he had delayed rearming because such an appeal would have lost him the general election.

Churchill urged on March 14, 1938, a guarantee for Czechoslovakia: "To English ears the name of Czechoslovakia sounds outlandish. No doubt they are only a small democratic state, no doubt they have an army only two or three times as large as ours, no doubt they have a munitions supply only three times as great as that of Italy, but still they are a virile people; they have their treaty rights, they have a line of fortresses, and they have a strongly manifested will to live freely." These were facts, and many asked why Mr. Chamberlain, when giving his melancholy broadcast at the height of the September crisis in 1938, described Czechoslovakia to English ears as "a faraway country of which we know nothing."

Churchill ended this same speech with a great plea for collective security: "If a number of states were assembled around Great Britain and France in a solemn treaty for mutual defense against aggression; if they had their forces marshaled in what you may call a Grand Alliance; if they had their Staff arrangements concerted; if all this rested, as it can honorably rest, upon the Covenant of the League of Nations, in pursuance of all the purposes and ideals of the League of Nations; if that were sustained, as it would be, by the moral sense of the world; and if it were done in the year 1938—and, believe me, it may be the last chance there will be for doing it—then I say that you might even now arrest the approaching war."

It was not done. Appeasement was preferred to the Grand Alliance. All know the consequences. In the spring of 1939 the British government began feverishly struggling to carry out the policy which Churchill had pressed upon them twelve months before.

On March 24, 1938, Chamberlain issued a warning but gave no guarantee. Churchill in his speech on that subject used a metaphor which gripped the imagination of his hearers: "I have watched this famous island descending incontinently, fecklessly, the stairway which leads to a dark gulf. It is a fine broad stairway at the beginning, but after a bit the carpet ends. A little farther on there are only flagstones, and a little farther on still these break beneath your feet."

Two last quotations. The "settlement" of Munich came in September, but Churchill was not to be deceived. In a speech on October 5th he observed that our hearts went out to the German people, but they had no power: "There can never be friendship between the British democracy and the Nazi power, that power which spurns Christian ethics, which cheers its onward course by a barbarous paganism, which vaunts the spirit of aggression and conquest, which derives strength and perverted pleasure from persecution, and uses, as we have seen, with pitiless brutality the threat of murderous force."

Churchill ended: "Do not suppose that this is the end. This is only the beginning of the reckoning. This is only the first sip, the first foretaste of a bitter cup which will be proffered to us year by year unless by a supreme recovery of moral health and martial vigor we arise again and take our stand for freedom as in the olden time."

Half a year had barely passed before Hitler tore up the Munich agreement and marched into Prague. And within another six months Britain and Germany were at war.

It could hardly be wondered at if the members of the government used to stir uneasily on the Front Bench when Winston Churchill strode into the House of Commons; nor that they were reluctant to give him their confidence and the responsibility of high office. Events have shown that on the cardinal issues of policy he has been right for the past five years and they have been wrong.

Today he is as big a man as any other two members of the Cabinet taken together.

Winston Churchill's private life is as admirable and as versatile as his public career. In both spheres he must be doing, making, constructing something. So he is an enthusiastic amateur bricklayer. By this craftsmanship he improves the amenities of his country house in Kent. That home is a retreat. The telephone number of Chartwell is a secret known only to his friends. He is the best of hosts and can so completely put guests at their ease that even quite young men are encouraged to call this formidably distinguished personality "Winston."

His wife is tall, handsome, smiling, aristocratic. She has kept her youth. Their family include a young man well known in the United States, Randolph, named for his grandfather. Randolph has great powers of speaking. He has on several occasions stood for Parliament as an Independent Conservative to the irritation of the official Conservative authorities. Once his intervention caused the election of a Socialist!

To Randolph, Winston is more of a brother than a father. After one of Winston's more volcanic explosions he was met by his son in the lobby of the House of Commons. Randolph seemed bent on some private destination. But Winston, human being from top to toe, needed the comfort of his son's presence. "Don't you go away," he said.

The fact that one of his daughters has married a song writer, Mr. Vic Oliver, would please him. All he would say is "Let her be happy." Another of his daughters is married to a rising young member of Parliament, Mr. Duncan Sandys.

Amid the splendors of the coronation of George VI,

Mr. and Mrs. Churchill revealed their difference of out-look. We were kept in Westminster Abbey for over six hours. Not only was it necessary to be there in gorgeous and uncomfortable apparel nearly four hours before the ceremony began, but the service itself lasted for hours. Directly it seemed that we were about to be released, there were Winston and his wife anxious to leave and somehow near the head of a queue near a door. Mrs. Churchill was smiling greetings to scores of friends. But Winston was intent on one thing. He wanted to get away from the crowd. Perhaps he needed to stretch his legs. More likely he was bent on getting to his study. He wanted to commit to writing while they were fresh his impres-sions of that astonishing pageant of color and ceremonial.

Though he then held no official position, his seat had been a prominent one far from an exit. But when the moment for departure came Winston was somehow in front. This little incident shows his capacity for being ahead of others. When he has something to do he will not waste time or allow others to get in his way.

As soon as he got home, I have no doubt, he cast aside the brilliant uniform which he had had to wear and put on his oldest and most comfortable clothes. He would eat quickly and well and at the earliest convenient mo-ment would get behind a stupendous cigar whose length would compete with his own shortish stature. He would march over to a desk where he is wont to write without sitting down. Standing there, he would pour out onto the paper before him a narrative whose poetic brilliance would outshine forever the more pedestrian efforts of the journalists who had laboriously and inadequately struggled to depict the same scenes.

Winston Churchill is back at the center of power and

responsibility. Once again at the opening of a campaign against Germany he was first lord of the admiralty. It was a strange experience for him to sit in Admiralty House again after a quarter of a century. He found himself moving over the same course, against the same enemy, in the same months of the year. It was, in his own words, "the sort of thing one would hardly expect to happen." In September he not only held the office he had occupied at the beginning of the First German War in 1914. He was also a member of the Inner War Cabinet of nine. His job was not limited to the control of a great and expanding navy. Along with eight others he was directly responsible for our policy in the war. That superb brain and that buoyant spirit had not only to direct his country's triumphant survival of disasters such as the sinking by enemy submarine action of the liner *Athenia*, of the aircraft carrier *Courageous*, and of hundreds of thousands of tonnage vitally necessary to our island's sustenance. That might be considered a task severe enough for any one man. But Churchill shares also in decisions upon the conduct of all hostilities by ourselves and in the framing of our war aims. To be first lord of the admiralty is for any man a full-time job. Many critics say he should be relieved of departmental cares so that he can concentrate on the general supervision of the campaign. Yet he may be big enough to do both duties.

When he was lately summoned back to the Admiralty he was in the midst of an immense work on *The History of the English-Speaking Peoples*. You might think it would have to be suspended till Germany is defeated, but you may be wrong. Probably Winston will go on with this work—and with an account of the present war—whenever he is able to take a few hours' recreation from his present

British Combine Photo

Winston Churchill (right), First Lord of the Admiralty, and Anthony Eden (left), Secretary of State for Dominion Affairs, with his wife, hold an impromptu conference after a recent Court function. Churchill, the vigorous head of Britain's naval might, is more hated and feared by the Germans than is any other member of the Cabinet. Eden, once the cause of a serious political upheaval, is now experiencing the confirmation of his predictions of a few years ago.

naval labors. What is toil to most men is refreshment to this magnetic genius.

Always thrusting forward, constantly acting on his own unauthorized initiative, these are the secrets of his renown for action. When in 1914 it was clear that Germany would go to war and that we must join France against her, Lord Fisher, first sea lord, said to the young first lord of the admiralty, "You must mobilize the fleet before you leave this room." When Winston complained that he had no authority from the Cabinet, Fisher asked him whether his career or the safety of England mattered more. Winston gave the order to the fleet.

Twenty years ago Winston still played a game where qualities of push-and-go and courage were vital. Even after the Great War he used to sweat and strain on the polo field. As he cavorted about he could recall the cavalry charges in which he had participated under Kitchener. To strike a polo ball must have seemed less exciting than to transfix a dervish.

There is no man better equipped to ensure victory for the Allies. There were few men as likely to stave off the calamity of war itself. It is hardly probable that Mr. Chamberlain, now seventy years of age, will last the whole course of a long war. If a fresh captain is needed, will the hand of Winston Churchill be brought to the helm? So tight is his grip now upon the public imagination that before these words are printed he may be prime minister.

Is he to be recognized for his wise and absorbing patriotism? Or is he to be penalized for his countless indiscretions? Will the Socialists forget his mortal assaults upon their policy and personnel? Several years ago the Trades-Union Congress passed a resolution opposing the rearmament of Germany. In the House of Commons,

Churchill quoted this opinion and then barked out, "What is going to prevent her rearming? A card vote of the T.U.C.?" Has moderate opinion forgiven his Indian antics and his personal and public anguish before the abdication of Edward VIII? Will the diehards accept him, or do they cherish the discredited ineptitudes of isolation? Can they really wish us to be, in Churchill's own language, "edged and pushed farther down the slope in a disorderly expostulating crowd of embarrassed states"? Will the true prophet forever be without the supreme honor of national leadership, and, by a cruel anticlimax, will he be kept from the highest office in the moment of Britain's direst need with the shallow and ignorant taunt, "What you lack is judgment"?

The answer may be known by the time this chapter has been published.

CHAPTER IV

LORD HALIFAX
Stern, Saintly, and Sly

CERTAIN families with a tradition of government enjoy a prescriptive claim to office in Great Britain. Chatsworth, Hatfield, Knowsley—Cavendish, Cecil, Stanley—these places and these names still dilate upon the canvas on which is pictured the government of Britain.

The feudal aristocracy has made itself thoroughly popular and has preserved the greater part of its privilege. The English—and the Scottish—will heed the scion of a noble house. If he exhibits any signs of sense, they will hang on his words. And if he has more than average wisdom, they will spontaneously look to him to lead and to govern.

This predisposition is not restricted to the British Conservative party. The writer has often heard normal working-class Socialists refer without any rancor to "those who govern us." There is an accepted governing class. It consists of the peerage and their immediate relatives. If that is a snobbish assertion, truth must be a snob.

During several periods within the twentieth century it has been the unchallenged fashion in Britain to say, "Of course, we shall never again have a prime minister in the House of Lords." Cynics have sharpened their wits at the expense of the "Upper House." "The Lords," it has been said, "are a dull lot. Recently a man was raised

83

to the peerage who was so dull that after a time the others began to notice it." And there is the story of the noble lord who dreamt that he was speaking in the House of Lords—and, when he woke up, he was!

The late Marquess Curzon, at one date viceroy of India and later foreign secretary, was ambitious to attain the highest pinnacle of fame. He just missed being prime minister. He wept; but comforted himself by the reflection that he was unfortunate in having been born a peer. Whether that circumstance in fact kept him down is perhaps merely a matter for charitable conjecture. Curzon seemed too far removed from the appetites and aspirations of ordinary men. Baldwin, who posed so successfully as the "plain, blunt, honest Englishman," was fortunately preferred to Curzon.

Today any rule there may have been is no longer exempt from challenge. There is a substantial possibility, amounting in the minds of some to likelihood, that before very long we shall see as prime minister Edward Frederick Lindley Wood, third Viscount Halifax.

It is further being predicted that the House of Commons might have, in those circumstances, to be "led" by Sir John Simon. That accessory would produce frustration and fireworks in approximately equal proportions.

The inconveniences of a prime minister in the House of Lords are numerous and obvious. He depends for his support on a majority in the Commons. He should be directly answerable to the elected representatives of the people. However good his sources of contact and information, only frequent presence in the chamber of the House of Commons will enable him to apprehend its mood, its temper, and its fluctuating affections.

This is said to be a democratic age; we all pretend that

it is. Even though leadership is to be found among those most richly endowed with the blessings of heredity and environment, we like to think that the king's first minister is a commoner like most of the rest of us.

For many of the same reasons it is not an ideal arrangement to have a foreign secretary out of the Commons. He is the minister of peace—and of war. Today war means jeopardy for all citizens. Normally citizens would like their elected members to be able to support, oppose, question, and defy the minister upon whose skill depend their chances of survival.

But once again, at a moment of emergency, the foreign minister is a peer. The arrangement has not had all the disadvantages that were predicted for it. Chamberlain shouldered his task of speaking for the Foreign Office in the Commons with the enthusiastic self-confidence of the amateur.

Alone among Cabinet ministers, it seems that the chancellor of the exchequer will be steadfastly found in the Commons. The Lower House has enjoyed since 1911 complete control of finance. "No taxation without representation" was a principle which the Boston Tea Party began to teach us. Seven score years later we had learned the lesson so thoroughly that it found its way into the Constitution at Westminster! A budget statement cannot, so long as our Constitution retains its present main features, be made to any other audience than the House of Commons.

What peculiarities of circumstance and character have made Lord Halifax so considerable a candidate for the office of prime minister? They are much the same as those which made him foreign secretary. He denies that he had any desire to supersede Anthony Eden. Indeed, it is likely that he shrank from the task. But there was really nobody else. Winston Churchill analyzed all the other possible aspirants in a speech of memorable satire, in which he dismissed the next most probable candidate, Sir Samuel Hoare, in a phrase: "Once bitten twice shy."

The schoolboy outlook persists with the politician, who is always unconsciously assimilating fresh impressions. The politician has learned the need for a certain minimum of toleration, so his cruelty is less gross and less persistent than that of the adolescent. But he rejoices in inventing sobriquets and impieties for men of special eminence; not all of them are flattering or good-natured. So Lord Halifax has become "The Holy Fox."

"An enemy hath done this," for this impious nickname is cleverer than any of those which invention and research have sought to attach to Mr. Chamberlain. Call a good man "holy" and he may be turned from a saint into a prig. And the fox, of all the animal kingdom, is adjudged to be most crafty at concealing its cunning course. The most damaging suggestion against Halifax would be that his virtuous exterior hides a dark and designing soul.

But with Lord Halifax any such accusation would fly wide of the truth. He cannot be accused of a shred of priggishness or a vestige of hypocrisy. Anything he said would be felt: most of the things he feels he finds himself able to say. Nor has he any tricks, foibles, or mannerisms to encourage more or less friendly caricature. Therefore, contemporary critics retreat before a character and a personality that are impregnable.

Thirty years hence, some literary descendant of Lytton Strachey may take it upon himself, by fresh flights of imagination and scraps of doubtful history, to blacken our more virtuous contemporaries for the entertainment of an inquisitive posterity. He will need to work hard to make any mud stick on Lord Halifax: in the language of the police court, nothing is known against the prisoner.

"The Holy Fox," however, has this further element of subtlety. Lord Halifax enjoys fox hunting. His left arm is withered, but that handicap does not keep him from the hunt. He is a gentle man, and if he could be intellectually convinced that hunting is cruel he would never hunt again. Has he ever stopped to analyze the inspiration of the chase? The answer must be "No." He instinctively accepts the thrilling English institution of fox hunting as he would automatically accept the duty to give a lady companion the wall.

He once said, "I would rather be a master of fox-hounds than premier." The first ambition he realized in 1932 when he was chosen master of the Middleton Hunt. This office, with its curiously great social prestige, he held till he was obliged to give it up in 1938 through pressure of public business.

Halifax has an impressive academic background. After Eton and Christ Church College, Oxford, he became a "Fellow of All Souls," the society which likes to pride itself on its intellectual dominance of the realm. Oxford has kept her hand raised to the salute, for in 1933 she made him her chancellor, the suggestion being that she regards him as quite one of her most distinguished off-spring.

Baldwin, whose academic interests were arrested in their development and were eventually eclectic, enjoys the same honor at the hands of Cambridge. Lord Baldwin was thrice prime minister. For the analogous honor—a great one at both of the chief English universities—Halifax is qualified by scholarship as well as statesmanship.

In 1910, aged twenty-nine, the Honorable Edward Wood became member of Parliament from Yorkshire, conveniently near to his family's territorial interests, and kept this seat for fifteen years. In 1937, aged twenty-five, the Honorable Charles Wood, son of the present Lord Halifax, was elected by the constituency of York. When the Second German War began he rejoined his regiment at once.

The father sat on the Conservative back benches in Commons till the First German War. Already he had begun to impress that turbulent assembly by his unflinching integrity. But he was a less exciting figure than the more active participants in violent conflicts between Liberals and Conservatives that distinguished prewar politics.

For those who came back there was an outstanding opportunity. They could posture as "old parliamentary hands" anxious to preserve in a shattered world and a mercantile collection of representatives those parliamentary privileges which had helped the House of Commons to function before the deluge. They had the advantage of an experience which had preceded Lloyd George's generous distribution of coupons at the general election of 1918.

Edward Wood sought to become an earnest guardian of all these important values. He took his parliamentary duties more seriously than ever, but he was so decorous that few dared to whisper "careerist." He was still a young hopeful, although in his late thirties.

I wonder whether Lord Halifax now regrets being numbered among those who urged Lloyd George at

Versailles to eschew clemency toward the vanquished. But his criticisms impelled him in another direction. He was one of the men who early discovered how futile was Lloyd George's Irish policy. Bloodshed merely begat fresh shedding of blood.

What was being done could be justified neither on Liberal nor on Unionist grounds. So Wood was as ready as anyone for negotiation, conciliation—and appeasement. He was in company as noble as himself. Lord Hugh Cecil and Lord Robert Cecil, brothers who were members of the House of Commons, drew their bows upon the prime minister.

While Neville Chamberlain moved obscurely on the back benches, Edward Wood kept himself to the front by assiduity of behavior and sincerity of attitude. Baldwin was attracted to him. He stood out physically and morally from the ranks of his shoddier colleagues. Moreover, he possessed that for which Baldwin has always fostered a predilection—high birth.

In 1921 Edward Wood was made undersecretary for the colonies by Lord George. But when Baldwin and Bonar Law slew the prime minister, Wood was as pleased as anyone; he joined the less experienced majority of Conservative rebels, ready for the administration of undiluted Conservatism. Austen Chamberlain, Birkenhead, and others of the more able men could not join the new government as they had openly sided with Lloyd George. Bonar Law was obliged to fill offices from the ranks of the undersecretaries. Edward Wood, in that moment of rocketing promotions, was made president of the Board of Education. He was thus in the Cabinet. He was officially assured of the larger audiences which his monumental dullness of manner had hitherto failed to attract.

When Baldwin came back at the head of a great majority in the winter of 1924 he remembered the saintly ex-president of the Board of Education. But now another aspect of his feudal background was to be honored, and he became minister of agriculture. The duty of presiding over the progressive decline of Britain's greatest industry was not to be pursued for long, for somebody had to be found to succeed Lord Reading, "the greatest Jew in Christendom," as viceroy of India.

Baldwin thought and blinked. What was he looking for? He wanted somebody who would pave the way for more reforms, who could enable the home government to make haste slowly, who could help Whitehall give Delhi the maximum of formal responsibility while conceding the minimum of decisive power. Someone was needed who would manage to impress the Indians with our sincerity, to whom all ideas of calling a colored people "damned niggers" were totally foreign, who could see wings prolonging the shoulder blades of all God's children, who had knowledge, culture, gentleness of manner, and incorruptibility of character.

Baldwin looked around his colleagues, and chose the noblest Christian in politics. Edward Wood exchanged the ministry of agriculture and fisheries for Viceregal Lodge.

For Baldwin's liberal purpose the selection was one of his more masterly strokes. Although it may have been a sort of snobbery which made him give Lord Irwin, as Wood now became, the whole of his confidence, Irwin was himself neither small enough nor imaginative enough to be a snob.

I do not believe that thoughts of racial differences or class distinctions for a moment enter his mind. He treats everyone as an equal with a naturalness more thorough than I have known in anyone else. There is no forced descent from some lonely eminence, no condescension to men of low estate, no hearty greeting with a noisy laugh or spurious embrace.

Halifax has exalted ordinariness; he is the incarnation of every beatitude. He is meek without cringing. His hunger after righteousness is plain to see upon his face. He is ready to show mercy to those rulers who least deserve it. It would be a blasphemy to charge him with a trace of impurity. And if he could find the way and could have his way, he would make peace. He is a real child of God.

He is good simply because it does not occur to him to be anything else. But as you talk to him you are not weighed down by any awareness of being in the presence of someone who is both great and good. You look into large eyes set in a placid face. His chin is not prominent and his mouth is of the wide variety that novelists call "generous." Of all the strange features, the upper lip is most characteristic. It proclaims its present nakedness of the mustache he once wore. He is at once in touch with you. If something slips from his lips that is clearly uncongenial to his companion his tact bids him steer away to a more sympathetic subject.

So the most sensitive Indian would be hard put to it to pick a quarrel. It is said that when as Lord Irwin he sailed for India his ship arrived on a Sunday, and he declined to disembark till the next morning. The Indians who understood are reported to have been favorably impressed. Here was a Christian who avoided unnecessary bustle and racket on his holy day.

His first meeting with Gandhi was without drama,

without ceremony, without recrimination, and without polemics. It opened the door to further negotiations. His policy was based on the theory that if he went on giving the other would grow tired of asking.

And so it proved. The Gandhi-Irwin conversations resulted in the decline of anarchy and in the approach to the conference table. Mr. Baldwin cordially endorsed what the viceroy was doing. He himself was having a rough passage with his own diehards.

Lord Irwin's term as viceroy had nearly run out, but Baldwin was in the middle of the sea. He was no longer prime minister, and the Indian policy he had inaugurated was in danger from a group in his own party. He obstinately declined to do what Churchill and his faction furiously desired—to lead an imperialist opposition to the Labor government's Indian policy.

In March, 1931, Baldwin decided to wash the Conservative linen in public, and he made a speech to which the House of Commons listened in a sort of pale silence. The diehards hated the oblique rebukes which he shot right home, but they sat in chilly self-discipline. It was the sensational utterance that wound up with this famous challenge: "If there are those in our party who approach this subject in a niggling grudging spirit, who would have to have forced out of their hands one concession after another, if they be a majority, *in God's name let them choose a man to lead them!*"

Earlier in the same speech he had been eloquent in his defense of Irwin. He deprecated the use of the words "victory" and "defeat" about the conversations between the viceroy and Gandhi: "Such a conclusion as has been reached could not have been reached by any other Englishman than Lord Irwin. It is a great tribute to his *char-*

acter—a character which has given him a prestige in India that nothing else could have afforded him. . . . The ultimate result depends, not on force, but on good will, sympathy and understanding between India and Great Britain; and the great work of Lord Irwin is that he has, after many years of suspicion, bridged the gap. He has bridged it by ability and character. . . . Five years is plenty of time for the best of us to make mistakes. Whatever mistakes he may have made, I am firmly convinced that, when the history of this time comes to be written, his name will stand out as that of one of the greatest viceroys, and a viceroy that I had the honor myself of sending to India."

Be it observed that Baldwin hardly troubled to argue; he merely asserted again and again his faith in Irwin's *character*. It is a character deeply embedded in religion.

The writer cannot presume to dogmatize on the truth or falsity of beliefs. Nevertheless, it is a truism that a man whose conduct is directed by a religious impulse is often happier and more effective merely because he is more confident. Even war itself, to a man of deep spiritual belief in the ultimate unreality of the things we now touch and see, loses half its grossness by losing all its terrors.

Lord Halifax is more than a mere believer; he is an institutionalist as well. He is an Anglican. The Church of England to which he adheres with such fidelity is divided horizontally by countless fissures. Roman Catholics might call them "schisms." While Lord Halifax himself does nothing fissiparous to add to the church's renown for standing every sort of doctrinal strain, he is to be found on the topmost layer. He is as "high" as his own head.

Halifax's life proves that an observer of elaborate ritual can keep his simplicity of soul. Only some lack of popular passion in his sermons could have kept him, if he had been ordained, from the summit of the Anglican hierarchy. While he was making a speech of specially righteous sentiment in the House of Lords, an elderly listener in one of the galleries sniggered to his neighbor, "He'd have made a good bishop!"

So be it; but not all English bishops have been bad men or incompetent men. Put William Temple, the archbishop of York, in charge of the Ministry of Health and Hensley Henson, the former bishop of Durham, into the Foreign Office, and you would face a bracing period of government. So, too, Edward Halifax's spotless virtue has not lessened his ministerial competence.

After a brief interval of rest on his return from India he became again, at the invitation of Ramsay MacDonald, president of the Board of Education. In him education united with uprightness, though there was a momentary fear lest the secondary schools might be sacrificed to economy. Critics have displayed a curious ignorance in some of their criticisms. When Baldwin became prime minister again there was a general shuffling among the elect. Halifax went to the War Office, at a moment when ideas of *la guerre totale* were still deemed to be ridiculous, and when the British Army was hardly to be taken seriously.

After the 1935 election he was relieved of departmental duties and, first as lord privy seal and then as lord president of the council, he acted as leader of the House of Lords. The serenity and somnolent calm of that august assembly were secure in his keeping.

Before the Eden crisis Halifax was to be the cause of a

strange episode. He went to Germany in the autumn of 1937 ostensibly to view a hunting exhibition. General Goering was his host, and an incredulous public was asked to believe that the expedition was devoid of political significance.

The poison began to work at once. It seems that Goering is capable of making himself agreeable. Like a master he employed with his noble visitor the method then practiced by the Germans in their contacts with Englishmen. Halifax was made heartily at home.

At once the charity that is always near the surface convinced him that Goering was quite a good fellow. His cruelties were obscured, if not quite forgotten. Halifax, intent on seeing anything that could even remotely be confused with goodness, did not perceive the escaped megalomaniac.

He saw, instead, a great fat egoist overflowing with his own importance, relatively free from physical fear, not without some vestiges of breeding or a certain gross humor, with a childish love of ostentation. "Humor him," whispered the voice of Christian charity; "if you stroke him he will purr and hide his claws." Thus did Halifax become *persona grata* to a man whom the best judges have called the least objectionable member of a government of criminals.

What passed between them is not public property. But we may infer that when Halifax returned to report to Neville Chamberlain, his current master, he expressed at least a mild amusement in his new acquaintance. Goering was not described as a creature of appalling potentialities; he was one who shared the psychology of other men. In this hopeful state of mind Halifax succeeded Eden in March, 1938.

Munich and its antecedents did not mean to him what they meant to Neville Chamberlain. The stripping of the defenses of Czechoslovakia, the flight of the Czechs and Jews from the Sudetenland, the possible consequences to the remnant of the republic were much more prominent in the conscience of one whose religion enjoined care for all who might fall into great tribulation. He soon revealed that he did not hail the "settlement" as a triumph of the new diplomacy; to him it was at best the lesser of two frightful evils.

When, in mid-March, Hitler rounded off in Prague his victory at Munich, it was generally believed that Halifax was better prepared for the shock than the prime minister. For he had the right formula ready. The speech he made five days after the German troops entered Prague caused a political commotion. The setting was a House of Lords unwontedly filled with peers who knew that, on this occasion at all events, they would be flattered by hearing something of importance.

The foreign secretary defined the purposes of Munich and then endeavored to meet the charge of having too guilelessly believed Hitler's assurances. The formula ran as follows: "No member of His Majesty's government has failed at any moment to be acutely conscious of the difference between beliefs and hope. It was surely legitimate and right to have hopes." The implication apparently was that Halifax believes only in things eternal. For his fellow men he cannot cherish any more stalwart emotion than hope.

The House of Lords, for some reason, contained a far higher proportion of pro-Germans than the House of Commons. On the whole, they are more interested in property, and to them the great menace to private owner-

British Combine Pho

Sir John Simon, Chancellor of the Exchequer, "director of Great Britain
invincible army—the army of pounds and shillings," is generally con
sidered to have the keenest mind in the war cabinet. He is the most di
tinguished lawyer in England, the deputy leader of the House o
Commons, but the least popular of statesmen.

ship lies in the Communism of Moscow. This simple
creed was exploited with brilliant success by the racket-
eers in Berlin. They claimed to be the great barrier to
the march of anarchy and depredation. A dangerously
high proportion of politically-minded noblemen have
lapped up this propaganda and longed to cuddle up to
the Nazi barrier against Bolshevism.

Consequently, some of their lordships must have heard
Halifax with deep searchings of their noble hearts. They
saw the barrier being finally exposed as a monstrous sham,
a fragile, transparent sheet of glass. What they can have
felt when Hitler and Stalin made their compact in August
is beyond the imagination.

Halifax eulogized the habit of his fellow countrymen
to want to shake hands after a scrap. Versailles contained
mistakes, but German action had persisted in making
progress to understanding more difficult. The latest
behavior of the Nazis had made economic collaboration
impossible. It required all free peoples to think out their
attitude anew. Which way should Britain now turn?

There were, Halifax argued, two possible courses to
pursue in the search for security and the avoidance of
war. There was the course laid down in the Covenant of
the League. By it all willing states accept the obligation
that an attack on one should be treated as an attack on all.

The second course was followed by those who held that
this collective security involved risks which greatly exceeded the safety it conferred; they thought that states
should bind themselves to intervene only in conflicts
where they were directly attacked. If the probability of
direct attack seems low, then a larger number of people
will incline to this second view.

But if, ran his argument, there is no apparent guarantee

against a succession of attacks directed on all states which seem to stand in the way of the march to domination, "then at once the scale tips the other way." Self-defense might seem to dictate the acceptance of wider mutual obligations in the cause of mutual support.

This weighty and elaborately argued inclination toward collective security, a thesis which I have telescoped into a few sentences, encouraged a number of people to jump on to the scales on the side to which Lord Halifax was clearly leaning. His speech made all the more impression because it followed at a short interval an icy douche from Sir John Simon discouraging just such a notion of wider obligations.

Eden and Churchill put down a resolution supporting Halifax's policy and urging a far greater effort of rearmament. About thirty more or less important names were added to the resolution. At once the government circles bridled. This specific approval of Halifax and what he had said was rather irrationally held in some quarters to be an attempt to embarrass Chamberlain, if not to betray and expel him from the premiership!

It was as though men did not know that a foreign secretary was supposed to speak the collective mind of the Cabinet. How could Halifax's speech have been made without Cabinet consultation of a particularly strenuous and unusually fruitful kind? Poland, Rumania, Greece, and Turkey were speedily guaranteed and conscription was introduced. The offending resolution, which did no more than accelerate or anticipate the government's decision, was obligingly withdrawn.

How Lord Halifax felt while making the effort to link arms with Moscow, which must often have seemed to him to embody Antichrist, baffles conjecture. In the light of his behavior as viceroy of India, one is inclined to think that he approached the job with less prejudice than a goodly proportion of his colleagues. Perhaps he would have preferred to mollify Goering and Hitler rather than bargain with Maisky and Molotov. But Halifax's bitterest critics cannot call him a stupid man, so, when the first policy became impossible, the second line might almost have seemed decent and desirable, lest the two enormous powers should unite to the disaster of Western Europe. It is hardly to be imagined that Halifax could swallow the propagandist nonsense which alleged that the Union of Socialist Soviet Republics was militarily a thing of straw.

In the summer of 1939 it became clear that there was a price for an alliance between Russia, on the one hand, and France and Great Britain, on the other. That price was British acquiescence in the virtual loss of their independence by the Baltic States to Russia. Halifax decided that such an acquiescence would not be honorable. When Germany was successfully battering Poland, Russia took by agreement with Hitler what she had desired to take by agreement with Halifax.

Such, then, is the God-fearing nobleman whom many are busily trying to groom for stardom. His record and his character are impressive, but his speaking is so unexciting and soporific that the public may look to him in vain for the heady stimulant of democratic eloquence. The proper specific could be supplied by some of the men who might be his first lieutenants, for Lord Halifax has incurred no personal enmities and could act as head of a ministry of various and competing talents.

Like Baldwin, Halifax would unite and not divide. "It is high time," say some, "that we again had a prime minister in the Lords, where he would be exempt from the rough-and-tumble of the Commons. What better sounding board could be found for the careful utterances of the one man upon whose least word such awful issues depend?" Thus, no doubt, can the snub which may be in store for representative government be speciously embellished.

Not only has Halifax allowed his generally temperate habits to govern his tongue, but his public manners are as courteous as his private deportment. His attitude on the Front Bench in the House of Lords indicates his whole outlook of unprejudiced inquiry. Whether the speaker is supporter or critic, he will peer intently over the top of his spectacles, keenly attentive to detect and appreciate anything valuable or constructive. The ankle of one long leg rests on the knee of the other, supporting the pad on which he is diligently noting points to blunt, to sharpen, or to dock.

As Halifax gazes at the noble orator his brow is furrowed in the anxious hope that the one who is now speaking will do himself full justice. Lord Halifax is too well schooled to smile or sneer. In the same mood and the same attitude when contemplating the personnel of less civilized governments than our own, he eagerly waits for some human monster to turn toward him any virtues he may possess.

In this setting he is seen at his best—the earnest seeker after the good in other men. To few of these human souls could his advance to the premiership cause deep distaste. But how many of them can see in the large and gentle being the kind of prime minister who might have to lead the nation through the final stage of the fiery test of war?

CHAPTER V

SIR JOHN SIMON
Searchlight on Westminster

THE keenest mind in the War Cabinet is that of Sir John Simon. He is by far the most distinguished lawyer in Britain. The conventional goal of an English lawyer's ambition is the woolsack, on which the lord chancellor sits when presiding in the House of Lords. Simon could have reached it on scores of occasions for a mere hint. But he has preferred to remain a member of the House of Commons. Why? In order, men say, to give himself the best chance of reaching the premiership to which his superb qualities might seem to entitle him.

At the moment he is chancellor of the exchequer. He is also deputy leader of the House of Commons. He has had to introduce a war budget whose taxation will, if it is maintained for any considerable period of time, fatally impair the comfort enjoyed by the "upper middle" classes. The payment in income tax of seven shillings and a half out of every twenty earned on incomes above a comparatively low figure is a Herculean burden. In the current year the war will cause national expenditure to approach ten billion dollars. Most of it is to be met by taxation. The population of the United Kingdom is less than fifty million.

That, in brief, is the problem before Sir John Simon. One would say that anyone who successfully mastered it would have some claims to be the next prime minister. But, for reasons which I am going to submit, Sir John Simon's chances are remote.

He has an intellect like a sword. His character is immaculate and incorruptible. He is the perfect lawyer. But he is among the least popular of statesmen. And when it has been necessary to make vital decisions he is possessed by a fatal indecisiveness. A member of Parliament once observed, "Don't imagine it's easy to be a politician. Just try sitting on the fence with one ear to the ground."

Simon, so his detractors say, has often taken this uncomfortable and impossible position. Another mixer of metaphors once said of him, "John Simon has sat on the fence so long that the iron has entered into his soul!"

He owes his present important positions not so much to his many good qualities as to powers as an advocate which made him an almost indispensable asset to the National government. Few characters are so dark that he cannot find some redeeming feature. Few mistakes are so gross that he cannot vest them with some slight attributes of wisdom. These exercises inspire admiration for his subtlety as well as grateful applause from a party anxiously searching for a dialectical exit from dense thickets. But they do not kindle personal affection or deep respect.

Approach the person of Sir John Simon. He is said to radiate physical coldness. You must sail as boldly as you can up to the edges of the iceberg. There you will spend a few chilly moments until you can proceed into warmer waters. Your problem of escape may be solved by the incalculable motions of the berg itself. It may suddenly sweep away before the impulse of some powerful and unpredictable eddy. You will be left floating and gasping.

But let us try to think of Simon as a man.

He will probably, it is said, look past you as he shakes hands. In that there may be little that is unjust. Have you his mind, his memory, his distinction? The chances are at least a million to one against you. But it is not an attractive greeting. Nor will you find it easy to carry on a light and amiable conversation. It will quickly develop into a monologue.

With great condescension Sir John will begin imparting information. If you venture to answer or attempt to make a positive contribution, beware of inaccuracies. You will be speedily put right. Anything like a discussion will be quietly scotched. Simon is deadly in argument and cannot resist one. He will annihilate any interchange by starting a disquisition.

You may think you are progressing well even though the gaze of the great one is straying over a picture or down the page of a book. He can listen and read at the same moment. Every weakness in your thought or language is being noted for the correction that is never long delayed. However slow your intelligence, you will soon be made to see how wrong you were or how incomplete your dialectical defenses. Thus Simon seeks to enliven the dullest company.

He may be surprised at the disappointing social consequences but he does not vary his manner. Has anyone dared to go to him and tell him with his own simplicity and directness that people do not enjoy being proved wrong or intellectually inferior? There is a belief that he yearns for friendship and friendliness. The only proof of this report is that in most men these are natural aspirations. Nor is there in his behavior any evidence that he really wants to be liked. I do not believe that he is capable of being so stupid as not to know that he goes the wrong way to win any kind of personal following.

Most men—above all, most politicians—enjoy an audience of the great. They like to be consulted, not squashed. He must know that. So the theory that his sudden assumptions of good-fellowship are due to a pathetic desire for the warmth of friendship is not wholly credible. The prayer to Providence that he may be made "a good fellow" is a legend, and not a plausible legend.

There is no evidence that Simon has any consciousness of imperfection. On the contrary, the notorious arm linkings and accostings of the unknown by wrong Christian names are—in so far as they occur at all—occasional lapses into a democratic deportment for which essentially he has no use. That they are ever tried is embarrassing; that they are so rarely performed is proof that at heart he despises them. He is perfectly at home in the chilly element that surrounds him.

A few years ago Simon still looked a young man. Now he is aging, but with great dignity. He is tallish and almost distinguished. His face is nearly handsome. It is not quite a photograph of virtue. It just fails to be very attractive. With a few adjustments he could be a bishop, with a few more a banker. Around his bald dome cluster tufts of woolly white hair. Today he is venerable as well as formidable; a few years ago he was merely terrifying. Now he mellows, ripens, and refuses to decay. He is still able to hop about like a man in his twenties. Age is treating his physique kindly. His face is still that of an opponent who will give no quarter. A hard chin, approaching the dimensions of that of the actor, Mr. Richard Dix, supports a mouth that seems fitted for sarcasm and denunciation. Above his red cheeks rove dark-brown eyes always reluctant, save when a crushing rhetorical question is uttered, to transfix a fellow human being.

In its way Simon's manner of speaking is unexceptionable. Thin but natural, his voice can be heard everywhere without effort. He has quaint habits of tenderly massaging his back and fiddling with the buttons of his waistcoat. Again, his large hand will stray toward his heart, and then the House prepares itself to hear some admirable sentiment.

With a devastating logic Simon can destroy the most sincerely and most ardently presented arguments. And he does the job with an effortless simplicity and a superiority of manner that depress opponents. Therefore, it is hardly to be wondered at when his critics indignantly protest that he could with equal facility make the opposite plea. Did not his annual emoluments when he practiced law represent a normal rate of interest on a capital of five million dollars? And the source of these princely riches was advocacy, nothing more.

He is now responsible for raising unheard-of amounts of revenue to defray the defense bill. Great armaments mean dangerous days. And these dangerous days have followed his three and a half years at the Foreign Office. *Post hoc propter hoc?* How lightly would Simon expose and riddle the fallacy! "Did I incite Japan to invade Manchuria? Did I inspire the Germans to cry 'Heil Hitler'? Did I inject the virus of aggression into the veins of Mussolini?" Loud laughter would punctuate each sally.

But the historian, who is not interested in the opportune refutation of fictitious charges, will not be so conveniently turned aside. For all these calamities—above all, for the failure of the Disarmament Conference—critics will try to saddle John Simon with the blame.

The oft-cited delight of the Japanese delegate at Geneva at Simon's presentation of the Japanese case will not be readily forgotten; nor will his alleged lack of any policy to submit to the Disarmament Conference till Germany's temper boiled up into Hitlerism. When President Hoover made proposals for a cut of one-third in the armaments of all powers, Simon was only able to "express the government's sense of their profound importance."

Time oozed away while he remained at the helm. His tenure of the Foreign Office cannot be described as a success. When explaining the lead we had given in disarmament "to the edge of risk"—a phrase which, as his own creation, he used to love to repeat—he specified as one of our disadvantages at Geneva our lack of weapons to offer for scrapping. Is this an argument or an excuse? While it may be difficult to answer, it fails to convince. How like its author!

But he is still in the Cabinet, almost a historic model of oral efficiency. His office is in theory second only to the premiership in importance. But there is this curious truth, that normally a chancellor of the exchequer, if he confines himself to raising revenue and balancing the budget, may do little harm. He is not nearly such a power for evil as a foreign secretary. Yet is it anything but the height of irony that, as chancellor, Simon should be having to make his fellow citizens pay for the misfortunes which follow his years at the head of the Foreign Office?

Suppose the premiership were suddenly to fall vacant, John Simon is the man who in theory should succeed. Make that suggestion to anyone moving within the inner circles of politics. He will not cheer or smile; he will meditate. But it would be unwise to say that this succession cannot come to pass. There might be tactical advantages in having a "Liberal National" to succeed two Conservatives and an ex-Socialist at the head of a National government.

To what extent is Simon a Liberal? The late Lord Birkenhead described as "a foolish and malicious invention" the story that he and Simon tossed up as undergraduates at Oxford to see which side each of them should take in politics.

Simon's public life may help to discover his convictions. His residence at Oxford coincided with that of Hilaire Belloc and Birkenhead—then plain F. E. Smith. All three went some distance to fulfill their early promise. Hilaire Belloc, today the least known, may be preserved to fame the longest of all: the mark made by fine literature is narrow but deep.

So long as Smith survived in his Lucullan and luxurious arrogance, he and Simon, betweenwhiles at issue, expressed mutual admiration. A faint glow of tenderness seems to inform Simon's anecdotal references to "F.E." That emotion may with some justification be mixed with pity. Simon has never been so foolish—or so human—as to give way to physical self-indulgence. His present health and stamina are the reward of studious self-discipline.

In his youth he could not have had many opportunities for fine living. He was most fortunately bred in the household of a nonconformist minister. An agreeable trait in Simon was his devotion to his mother, who lived to a great age. John went to a famous Scottish school before proceeding to Wadham College, Oxford.

At Oxford he became, as did Belloc and "F.E.," president of the Union. The Oxford Union is the University Debating Society and is often described as a "nursery of statesmen." It demands and appreciates epigram. It is inclined to be impatient of the kind of argument at which Simon has always shone. So Simon's distinction is real evidence of great excellence. They also made him a "Fellow of All Souls," an honor denied to Birkenhead. No easy road to legal achievement lay before him. He assisted himself by winning the Barstow Law Scholarship and was called to the bar in 1899.

The legal profession in Britain is in two parts. Barristers, those called to the "bar" of the courts, have the right to plead in the High Court. Solicitors are those who prepare the documents. There are many other distinctions, but an important point is the practical difference that, whereas a solicitor can usually find enough work to give him a living, the bar is a gamble. On the other hand, great rewards and glittering prizes await the barrister who has patience, influence, ability, and courage.

He may spend years of suspense before any solicitor sends him briefs. So he keeps himself going by various devices. Simon has never written anything that people want to remember or preserve. But in his early days at the bar he was not above helping to boil his pot with the proceeds of journalism. Wise young man!

Early in his life he had to endure a tragic end to great happiness. He married at the age of twenty-six, but lost his wife in three years. He was terribly wounded by this cruel stroke. His wife left him with three children. For eighteen years Simon remained single pursuing a career with superhuman application. He married again in 1917. He now enjoys so much private happiness that all his energies are available for public work.

Simon "got on." In 1906, a youth of thirty-two, he entered the House of Commons as a Liberal. Four years later he was solicitor general. In 1913 he became the technical head of his profession by succeeding Sir Rufus Isaacs as attorney general. Sir Rufus Isaacs, as Lord Reading, was later to be viceroy of India and British ambassador to Washington. Simon was elevated to the Cabinet and, before the war, was sharing directly in the supreme responsibility of government. He was widely acclaimed as an unbending champion of free trade. Two more years passed during which he and his colleagues began the first war against Germany. The first Coalition was formed under Asquith. Simon became home secretary.

In 1916 came turning point number one. Asquith decided to introduce conscription. Simon's critics say that he believed the measure would prove an unpopular failure. His supporters say that Simon's conscience was touched on the raw. Compulsion of the individual on this issue was wholly objectionable to him. All that was Liberal within him rebelled. Not being a timeserver or a placeman, he resigned.

Nobody can say what went on within that superlative brain. If he expected a popular revulsion he made an immense miscalculation. I should prefer to attribute to Simon's move complete sincerity. It is the easiest explanation. It fits his earlier record. He could contend that compulsory military service was a denial of all for which the country was fighting, that no citizen of a free democracy had a right to impose this service on his fellows, and that what we should gain in numbers we should lose in good will.

The event did not support his third plea. But no one could foresee that. After the ides of March, 1939, there was a growing pressure on the government to leave nothing to chance in any collision with Germany. The demand was heard that every Englishman should be a conscript.

Indeed, its strength became so great that the Cabinet seemed in the dilemma of having to choose between quitting or submitting. They might have felt that to conscript our manhood would be to misdirect our energy. But they may also have regarded themselves as so precious to the nation that they must give way against their better judgment. It was wondered how Simon would behave. Would the evil of 1916, when Britain was threatened with defeat, become the stern necessity of 1939, when Britain was actually at peace? Fortunately, he changed his opinion. Conscription was introduced, but Simon is still there.

That was in 1939; but in 1916 out of the government went Simon and into the Royal Air Force. If he learned to pilot a machine he no longer practices that art. Somehow Simon is not to be associated with aerial stunts. He managed to do some work at the bar. But before long he was to suffer again.

The war ended. To his credit, Simon followed Asquith and not Lloyd George in the infamous election of 1918. Few candidates who neither breathed fire and slaughter against the German ex-emperor nor proposed that vast and unobtainable plunder should be squeezed from the vanquished stood any chance of survival. Two prominent slogans were "Hang the Kaiser" and "Make Germany Pay."

With Asquith Simon fought; with Asquith he fell. To suffer defeat at that election was a creditable thing. For Simon to have courted it, when he could have crept under the wing of the triumphant Lloyd George, was almost heroic. It is recorded—doubtless apocryphally—that before the war Simon had once been detailed to wind up an important debate for the government. He perambulated the lobbies describing his qualms. Of this kind of nerves

the statuesque Asquith was always supremely contemptuous. He observed to a companion, "There is a disturbance
in that which Simon is pleased to call his guts." But round
about 1918 Sir John was certainly showing a quality
which many would identify with courage.

It asserted itself again a little later. Lloyd George met
the Irish Sinn Feiners with reprisals. The "Black and
Tans" were formed as auxiliaries to the Royal Irish Con-
stabulary and were allowed to behave with a violence
which earned them the deepest disrepute. But for the
time England was more concerned with the atrocities of
the Irish Republicans. The burning of creameries carried
out by the Black and Tans seemed less savage than the as-
sassination of unarmed officers. And so it was. But it was a
stupid act to destroy a source of livelihood, and retaliation
by the Black and Tans did not end there. Simon mounted
platforms and exposed the folly and futility of Lloyd
George's policy. Sometimes his audience howled at him.
These experiences could have been neither to his taste nor
to his advantage. But events vindicated him fully.

He glided back into the House in 1922. During this
postwar period lasting till November, 1931, he is commonly understood to have earned unprecedented and unparalleled fees at the bar. But he also presided over the
Royal Commission on India, and that act of public service
must have reduced his chances of gain.

The dimensions of a man's earnings or winnings are
not as a rule interesting. But Simon was a prodigy. He was
so busy at the bar that clients who had to pay unheard-of
fees for consultations would boil with indignation at the
scant attention he seemed to be giving them. He would
stare at some point behind the expositor's head, or seem to
concentrate on a document while the solicitor stuttered in

his haste to reach the point, or he would hustle the whole bunch out of his chambers long before they felt satisfied. Then he would dictate a superb opinion or come into court and mesmerize judge, opponents, and hostile witnesses. While the judge was delivering his judgment Simon would begin perusing another brief. And each pile of documents would probably be marked "Sir John Simon 1,000 guineas."

His position at the bar was singular. If the judge seemed to exceed what Simon adjudged to be relevance he would utter a comment in an audible whisper to a neighboring king's counsel. These must have been happy years for him as he proceeded from court to court, fawned upon by the bar and feared by the bench.

In 1926 his advocacy proved of considerable value to the Conservative government. In the House of Commons he reinforced the judgment of Mr. Justice Astbury, who found that the general strike was illegal; that the action of the Trades-Union Congress was not protected by the Trades Disputes Act of 1906. This finding was to many as surprising as Simon's interpretation. But there is no doubt that the effect of Simon's exploits was to shorten the strike. Respectable trade-union officials did not fancy themselves as prodigal lawbreakers.

So these officials went to No. 10 Downing Street and settled the strike in the benevolent presence of Mr. Baldwin, who "thanked God for their decision." Simon was very pleased with himself. He had a little book printed called *The General Strike*. It contains his speeches on this strange and dangerous interlude, and includes as an appendix the terms of the Trades Disputes Act. You could read therein what in 1906 the term "trade dispute" was defined to embrace. And you could judge for yourself whether twenty years later John Simon was right. In any event, his advocacy was an element in our avoidance of bloody revolution. No shots were fired during nine days of strain. The collapse of the strike was as complete as the stoppage it had caused.

Such is part of the background to the fatal years 1931 to 1935. As the insolvent Labor administration was staggering to its doom, Simon associated more and more intimately with the Tories who were harrying its course. But he did not enjoy a scathless progress.

The main element of controversy in Snowden's budget of April, 1931 (not the later emergency budget), was the taxation of land values. On July 3rd, during the third reading of the Finance Bill, Simon contended that, although such taxation conformed with Liberal principles, the manner in which Snowden was applying it amounted to the early stages of confiscation. Simon was also known to be leaning to tariffs. When later in the throes of the financial crisis Britain had to leave the gold standard, Simon found further reasons for a discriminating tariff.

Lloyd George, supporting Snowden, was present that Friday noon to lead most of the Liberals into the division lobby in support of the Labor government. As Simon seemed to be turning his back on free trade and other Liberal principles, his fellow Welshman drew out his longest and knottiest scourge and lashed the apostate. Lloyd George left the chamber for a few minutes and after an intensive preparation returned to castigate the unfortunate. Here are a few gems of invective:

"To all who have been strictly orthodox there is a satisfaction in seeing the mighty fallen, a sort of naughty satisfaction. It is like the case of the teetotaler who all his life has been so stern that he looked with lofty disdain on anyone who took a drop of alcohol—however diluted—to his lips, and suddenly, when he is approaching the seventh decade of his life, he takes to drink: you see him reeling from one side to the other and he ends his career by entering an inebriates' home. . . ."

Lloyd George illustrated the drunkard's progress with all his resources of pantomime. But Simon was to be held up not only as an intellectual sot, but as a hypocrite as well:

"I do object to this intolerant self-righteousness. . . . Greater men have changed their opinions in the past, but they have never taunted those who still adhered to the underlying principle with lack of principle, with being mere maneuverers and tacticians. They, at any rate, did not leave behind *the slime of hypocrisy* in passing from one side to another."

Lloyd George, the crafty old parliamentarian, kept just within the rules of order as he stung his victim's cheeks from pink to crimson. Seldom has the House of Commons seen so terrible a denunciation. But the executioner ended with an even more pitiless stroke. Simon had rashly called the bulk of the Liberals his "lamented friends." Lloyd George cried:

"May I give him, as a lamented friend, a word of warning! The Conservative party will hail with rapturous delight his criticisms upon his friends and his attacks upon the causes to which they adhere. They will applaud him. They will use him to the utmost—all his powers and all his gifts—and when he ceases to be useful to them, they will fling him aside—or they will treat him as they treated an infinitely greater man, Mr. Joseph Chamberlain. They will fob him off with a second- or third-rate office, and cheat him of the prize which they dangled before him."

Lloyd George's analysis may have cast in relief all Simon's worst weaknesses. But as a prophet he was wrong. Within four months Simon had become foreign secretary.

Here was a man, three parts lawyer and one part politician, presented with an opportunity which comes once in a generation. A bold program of general disarmament might have been accepted and have secured civilization. Great results might have followed an active examination of the "Hoover plan."

But Simon depended upon a Conservative majority in the House of Commons which identified great armaments with national security. The vicissitudes of politics had elevated him to an office of matchless distinction. Which way should he set his course? Should he steer for the goal of universal safety and jeopardize his great position, or should be keep his office by giving his followers a transitory satisfaction?

Only Simon's blindest adversaries would say that he alone was the parent of the progressive worsening of world relationships. But there is the fact. And no one could charge him with failure to please the hundreds of Conservatives to whom disarmament was the height of folly. For three years and a half Simon kept himself in favor, till the failure of his policy was too obvious to be concealed by the brilliance of his debating. The reader of his speeches during his tenure of the Foreign Office will marvel at their consummate skill. The emphasis, the phrasing, the arrangement were all perfectly calculated to gratify those on whom he relied for support. Time and time again he would score a great triumph in the House of Commons and just as regularly the public would grow more and more apprehensive at the darkening of the sky. He turned corner after corner, but his path became stonier after each momentary respite.

Eventually the Conservatives themselves, by their private representations to the "whips" (the party members responsible for party discipline), and so to the government, showed that, while they might have cheered themselves hoarse, they were not blind to the lack of results. Simon was removed to the Home Office.

His speeches in Commons as foreign secretary reflected his great talent—and also revealed his weakness. He addressed the House as though it were a great jury. Here is how Simon did it. He is rebuking Sir Stafford Cripps, the Socialist ex-solicitor general, who has rashly committed himself to the remark that in disarmament Great Britain has "done nothing." Simon begins a crushing retort by the deliberate sentence, "The learned gentleman is too young"—pause while the government back benches rock with applause which Cripps must feel like a whip across his eyes.

Simon goes on to compare our armed forces with those we had at the Armistice in 1918! He then observes that Cripps is exhibiting a classic instance of "fouling one's own nest." More tumultuous and vengeful applause. But to gain this effect Simon has had recourse to the argumental device of confounding the government with the nation. Neville Chamberlain was later to employ this same expedient.

Once Simon caused such a disastrous impression that the House of Commons witnessed from him an approach to a public apology. It was in the autumn of 1934, when the public had been suffering from an acute attack of conscience upon the private manufacture of armaments. Mr.

Attlee, the Socialist, had mentioned the white-slave traffic, as well as the evidence before the American Commission on this same question. So when Simon spoke he said, "Let me ask the honorable gentleman: is it his view that state brothels are right but private brothels are wrong?" Several members of the little band of Socialists called out with irrational anger, "Dirty!"

After a long speech of dialectical excellence he included in his peroration two strikingly irrelevant quotations. The first was Sir Edward Grey's remark on August 3, 1914: "The lights are going out all over Europe; they will never be lit again in my lifetime." The other was from Thackeray's *Vanity Fair*: "Amelia was praying for George, who was lying on his face, dead, with a bullet through his head." This Simon described as "upon the whole the most moving single sentence in modern English literature."

Mr. Baldwin took care to "wind up" the debate as he shrewdly detected that this sort of pleading would be fatal if left unredeemed. Next morning *The Times* had a heading "Mr. Baldwin to the Rescue."

A fortnight later Simon nearly managed to kiss the rod when he said, "If a speech is to be judged, not by the exact words which are used, but by the impression which, I will not say it sought to create, but which has been created about it outside, well, then mine was a very unfortunate speech." But Simon, to keep pace with his misfortunes, should be ready to say "peccavi" not once, but many times. Seldom can a principal minister have climbed down so far and so soon. But he could not eradicate the impression.

Then there is his speech denouncing the arrest in Russia of the British Metropolitan-Vickers engineers. Russian ideas of justice may have deserved the sternest denunciation, and how Simon exulted as he thumped away! How appropriately his voice broke when he referred to the messages which the unfortunate men wanted to send to their wives and relatives in distant Albion! How he loved the applause raised by his appeals to prejudice! The massive Conservative representation could hurrah to their hearts' delight at the deadly scorn heaped on their adversaries.

One other exploit by counsel for the prosecution will live long in the memory of those who witnessed it. Mr. Winston Churchill had charged Sir Samuel Hoare with committing a breach of privilege by attempting to arrange the evidence to be given before the Joint Select Committee on India. The Committee of Privileges exonerated Hoare. In the subsequent debate Simon sailed in as champion of Hoare and castigator of Churchill.

"I begin to think," said Simon, with righteous indignation and appropriate majesty of language, "that these *proceedings* are not engineered in order to vindicate the law of Parliament . . . they were started in the hope and belief"—Simon frowned and raised his voice—"that they would bring upon my right honorable friend the secretary of state for India ruin!" The forensic eloquence waxed. "At the end of two months, during which he has endured this grievous charge and this great wrong, he is unanimously acquitted. Instead of the ruin which it was designed to bring upon him he has got his vindication. . . ." And so on. Simon gave a good exhibition of how this kind of thing can be done by an expert. Advocates might well copy Simon's perfection of technique. The great Churchill, sensitive and white-faced, sat angrily taking his medicine with muttered protests.

Immediately after the German invasion of Bohemia

in 1939 Eden, as a private member and former foreign
secretary, spoke strongly in favor of full military com-
mitments with all those nations who would join us. At
the end of the debate Simon defended the Chamberlain
policy, said it was to be continued, and argued that the
country would never sanction a commitment "which
might extend over half the world." He was elaborate in
his criticisms of our extending our automatic obligations.

Yet by April 3rd, after the guarantee to Poland, Simon
was able to say, "Accepting as we do, pretty well all of us,
this tremendous declaration and all that it involves, . . .
we will throw the whole potential strength of Britain into
this essential work. That strength must be used if need
be . . . to fight." No wonder prominent politicians often
say they are impressed with the speed at which things
move today.

The American writer, Ralph Waldo Emerson, is, of all
prose authors, the most "quotable." Simon has never been
guilty of that "foolish consistency" which Emerson says is
"the hobgoblin of little minds, adored by little statesmen
and philosophers and divines."

When sanctions against Italy were raised in June, 1936,
Lloyd George gave one of his most brilliant performances.
He quoted the government manifesto of the general election seven months earlier: "In the present unhappy dispute between Italy and Abyssinia, there will be no
wavering"—this word came out with a world of cunning
emphasis—"in the policy we have hitherto pursued."

Lloyd George went on: "But most important in that
document are the signatures. Their names are the guarantee that there could be no *wavering*: Stanley Baldwin"
(some laughter), "J. Ramsay MacDonald" (the laughter
began to become hilarious)—the prince of parliamentary

performers turned with a broad and wicked smile toward the best section of his audience—the Opposition Liberals —and then called out "John Simon!"

Great peals of laughter rose from everyone everywhere, the group of Liberals whom Simon had left, the other group of Liberals whom Simon was leading, the Tories whom he aspired to lead, and the Labor party who had never been so honored.

No doubt, Sir John will one day be blessed by a biographer who will do him more than justice. If the present writer has missed some noble quality he laments his own blindness.

There is certainly one evil that is said to rouse his deepest passions. It is slavery. Even in the twentieth century it still disgraces corners of the globe. On this subject Lady Simon, for whom Sir John never conceals his affection, has written a valuable work.

CHAPTER VI

ANTHONY EDEN
"Dear Anthony"

ON FEBRUARY 20, 1938, the world of politics was startled to learn that the Right Honorable Anthony Eden, aged forty-one, had resigned from the office of British foreign secretary. Two days later Winston Churchill celebrated his achievements. He said that Eden was "the one fresh figure of first magnitude arising out of the generation which was ravaged by the war." A Socialist who heard this pronouncement called out, "What about Hore-Belisha?" Mr. Hore-Belisha, who is not easily embarrassed, dropped his eyes in some confusion. It was not a very sensible interjection. Hore-Belisha is fully conscious of his own promise and performance. But few with any knowledge would rank him with Anthony Eden.

"The one fresh figure." Not for the first time, nor for the last, did Winston Churchill hit the mark. Britain is a country where youth is seldom served in politics. Eden has hardly had time to become shop-soiled or tarnished.

Three factors have made him renowned at such an early age: First, he possesses the inestimable advantages in Britain of good birth, wealth, and high connections. Second, he is a man of great knowledge and intelligence. Third, he is animated by intense seriousness of purpose.

Few backgrounds could be more conventional in an English sense. He is the son of a baronet and was sent to

school at Eton. His career then suffered the violent inter-
ruption which all his English contemporaries underwent.
Having been born in 1897, he was caught up in the war
in 1915. By 1919 he had won the Military Cross and had
risen to be a major. So, by the age of twenty-two he had
discovered at first hand the meaning of war. His hatred of
it was due not to cowardice, but to experience. He early
resolved to fight war with the weapons he thought sharp-
est. That war has come again is not due to any slackness
on the part of Anthony Eden. A French observer once
called him "This formidable young man who loves peace
so terribly."

At Oxford after the war Eden proved he had a first-
class intellect, undimmed by the explosions he had heard
and the carnage he had witnessed. Directly he left the
university he ran for election to Parliament. The year
after this unsuccessful attempt he was elected for a safe
Conservative seat where he can stay forever—always provided he remains loyal to Toryism.

Almost simultaneously with his election he married the
dark and graceful daughter of a wealthy banker and proprietor of the important provincial newspaper, the *Yorkshire Post*. When he died a year or so ago Mr. and Mrs.
Anthony Eden became still more independent of financial
worries. And Eden became even further removed from
having "anything to gain" by absorption in politics.

When I was in the United States some fourteen years
ago someone said to me, "You in England have more men
than we have who enter politics with the sole idea of serving their country." I refused—and still refuse—to accept
the notion that incorruptibility is the monopoly of the
statesmen of any one country. But Eden is certainly an
example of the man who is so detached from ordinary

anxieties and has already so high a social station that mere considerations of financial or social advancement are simply outside his experience. I am certain that there are many such men in the United States. It is equally true that England still abounds in them.

So reliable and intelligent a young man was likely to attract the eye of authority. From 1924 to 1929 Sir Austen Chamberlain was foreign secretary. In 1926 he selected Anthony Eden as his "parliamentary private secretary."

That is a wholly unofficial position. Every minister, whether in the Cabinet or not, takes as an unofficial assistant a "back-bench" member of Parliament. The selection may be due to the young man's charm or his ability. The value of his position varies with the importance of his chief's office and his own zeal for work. He has access to the secret department papers, and he is under no direct obligation to do any particular work. But in practice he sits in the House of Commons behind his chief and supplies him during debates with necessary documents and information.

If the minister is one of the heads of government, there is a great opportunity. He will consult the secretary and may even come to rely upon his advice and judgment. The position of parliamentary private secretary is often a steppingstone to office.

So it proved with Eden. Austen Chamberlain, the half brother of the prime minister from whom Eden was later to part company, formed a high opinion of the young man. He took him to Geneva when as foreign secretary he represented Great Britain. There Eden learned to value the infant machinery of the League of Nations. His agreeable personality made him a great success among foreign statesmen. Austen Chamberlain grew to trust him. Several years later when he had retired and Sir John Simon was foreign secretary, with Eden undersecretary of state for foreign affairs, Austen confessed that he was far happier when Eden was handling our policy.

In the autumn of 1931, MacDonald gave Eden his first office as Simon's lieutenant. From that moment to his resignation six and a half years later, he was continuously in office, either as undersecretary of state or as foreign secretary. He has greatly matured in the past eight years. But today he is still the fresh-complexioned Anthony Eden whom we knew before he had held office and when he was a young and little-known undersecretary.

Anthony looks a man who is on the best of terms with the open air. He is not a great athlete, but rejoices in seashore and mountainside as a release from the rigors of office. His physical characteristics play an important part in his career. He has a strange gait. He rolls slightly from side to side as he strides along like an earnest and amiable boy. He has been accorded a high place of honor among wearers of well-cut and expensive clothes. Yet his movements are so youthful and his body is so spare that he might well be wearing his first suit made to measure. If a malicious sprite were to clip off his mustache, he would almost shine out as an adolescent.

Perhaps he is self-conscious, and proud of his sartorial reputation. And a boyish trait is an obstinate inability to leave his mustache alone. It is an excellent military growth, but his fingers are always straying to his upper lip as though to explore a new symptom of manhood. He can be posed to yield an impressive photograph. If you knew nothing of the subject you would say, "Here is a handsome, bright-eyed young officer in the British

Army." But, thank heaven—and contrary to a popular conception—he would never excel as a film actor.

He is no schoolgirl's idol. A young maiden who had admired one of his boyish photographs would sustain a mild and wholesome shock when she met him. She would exchange a limp handshake with a man on whom the burden of office has left a deep mark forever. His forehead is heavily furrowed. His manner is serious. Serious, too, are his features without seeming strong; his chin might with advantage have been bigger. His smile is bright but not facetious. Seriousness quickly supervenes. His hair is beginning to be flecked with gray. If he was not wearing his glasses he would screw up his eyes to see his fan's face. Or he might peer at her through the heavy lenses of his spectacles. She would converse with a man of anxious and intellectual exterior who would need severe treatment from a make-up artist before he could safely walk the stage.

And then her preconceptions would suffer another blow. Whether they talked of the weather, or literature, or politics there would be no enchanting tones of voice, no resonant chords to suggest Gary Cooper, no tones that recall Bing Crosby; just a high-pitched, tired, faintly superior delivery.

Personally he is extremely agreeable. He has some tricks of manner which disarm companions. When asked a question he will drawl out a "What?" and thus give himself time to think when asked his opinion. It is an avuncular little sound, half pitying, remotely condescending. The typical English colonel is supposed to have no further vocabulary. Not so Major Eden. He can do much better when he is so minded.

He has culled a priceless device from the repertories of

Baldwin and Lloyd George. However dull or stupid or obscure his companion may be, he will invite his opinion as though it were worth having. Immediately the little person swells with self-importance and springs into top gear. He forgets that he is speaking to a man of deep knowledge and great experience; in a moment he is talking away to an apparently interested listener. He comes away with a profound sense of the intelligence, politeness, and charm of the statesman he has been lecturing. Thus do democratic leaders endear followers or create toleration for themselves among ever-widening circles.

Or, some unknown may feel a hand on his shoulder and, as he turns round, see the carefully groomed head and solicitous features. Eden may have a compliment to pay about a speech that was helpful or not too abysmally bad. Or he may have information to convey. This is usually done briskly, adequately, but with economy of phrase. The honored individual, especially if Anthony makes an appeal to his discretion, once more glows and vows abiding loyalty—for the time being.

Better than most ministers he could disarm the criticism of supporters and opponents. When he was foreign secretary he would readily take men into his confidence and explain why it was inopportune to raise this or that question about Manchuria, or the United States, or Italy, or Germany. He knows that a confidence is nearly always safe when the recipient is treated with candor and the respect appropriate to dealings among equals.

Not unlike Disraeli, he succeeded in educating his own party. While he was at the Foreign Office he was identified more and more in the public mind with an effort to make the League of Nations the instrument of a new international order. But the greatest skepticism prevailed among many of his fellow Conservatives. Some thought he was superb and the rising star of British statesmanship. Others waited and watched for the crash they thought must come.

Yet if Eden had been five years older and foreign secretary in 1931, the course of history might have been different. At Geneva personal amenity matters. To an exceptional extent, and better than most Englishmen, Eden knew how to charm the foreigner. Even the Disarmament Conference might not have failed, for Eden made things go smoothly when he was free from the presence of Sir John Simon. The policies which, during this period, achieved the solutions may not have been Eden's own, but to him, as spokesman for Great Britain, must go the main credit for settlement of the dispute between Hungary and Yugoslavia and for the international policing of the Saar.

Before Simon had been replaced by Sir Samuel Hoare in 1935, the storm was already brewing above Ethiopia. Eden seemed to be tying down Signor Mussolini and Baron Aloisi to a number of pacific declarations. But the Italian undertakings were not to be fulfilled. The Italian attack began and Eden became identified with Hoare's sanctions policy. An election was fought on high moral principles.

Early in December, just after the general election in Britain, Laval twisted the luckless Hoare into agreement with proposals which seemed a negation of those principles. Immediately Eden saw how detestably impossible the situation was. He was frantic with disgust. Mr. Baldwin's famous "sealed lips" did not prevent his swallowing Hoare's resignation. In January, 1936, at the age of thirty-eight, Eden, the minister for League of Nations affairs, became foreign secretary. I should hesitate to say that Eden's main interest is his own career and I am quite sure that he did not deliberately seek this particular bound forward. There seemed to be no one else for Baldwin to promote.

Eden was fortunate in his chief but profoundly unlucky in the course of events. Baldwin was so trusting, and so thankful for an excuse not to interfere, that he left his "blue-eyed boy" comparatively alone. But Hitler chose this moment to administer one of those shocks which Europe grew used to expecting from him. He occupied the Rhineland with his military forces. This act was a breach of the Locarno Treaty. According to the opinion of Austen Chamberlain, who negotiated the treaty for Great Britain, we were bound under its terms to come to the assistance of France in expelling the Germans from the demilitarized zone. It is not possible to say whether Eden shared that view, although in the debate three weeks later he said, "I am not prepared to be the first British foreign secretary to go back on a British signature."

The task of turning Germany out was at the moment well within the powers of France and Great Britain, and would have stemmed the progressive deterioration that flooded on so fatefully to Munich; but the signal to act did not come. Certainly there was no public demand for it. The public asked the simple question, "Why should not Germany put her own troops into her own territory?" Indeed, many simple folk, blinded as they were by the pro-German propaganda with which the press reeked, were inclined to applaud and shout, "Heil Hitler!"

In the summer sanctions against Italy were raised and

Eden stood sorrowfully amidst the havoc made inevitable by the proposals of Laval and Hoare. The principal preoccupation of the remainder of his period of office was the Spanish Civil War. He had one more triumph before Neville Chamberlain assumed full control—the Nyon Conference, under which submarine piracy in the Mediterranean was stamped out. For the moment collective action, the goal of Eden's endeavors which had been so often derided by the skeptics, stood out as the only method of ensuring sanity. The occasion of resignation and the atmosphere of the autumn crisis will be described directly. But first, a digression.

At the end of 1938 Mr. Chamberlain bestowed a blessing on Eden's entirely unofficial visit to the United States. It is said in England that this brief journey was a great success, and that the young women of America were vastly more demonstrative than their colder cousins in England. One confident prediction is now unlikely to be fulfilled. Eden will not become ambassador to Washington, at least not for many years. From the British viewpoint, Eden as a peer and an ambassador, and hence removed from active political service, would seem an anticlimax.

For the six years and a half that he was in office all the Conservatives hilariously cheered his more successful sallies against the Opposition. Some with enthusiasm, and others half in apprehension, acclaimed his regular and cautious flights into the realms of idealism. It is not beyond possibility that they might all form the habit of cheering him as their leader.

Support for this possibility can be found in many quarters. Plenty of Conservatives are shrewd enough to appraise Anthony Eden as a first-class electoral asset. He is widely regarded as one who has set a higher value on principle than upon office. There is in England a large nonconformist section, too small to form the substance of a party but big enough to turn the scale at a general election. This remnant, deriving from prewar Liberalism, deprecates the wilder enthusiasms of Socialism. They would not reject an excuse for voting for a Conservatism which is democratic enough and righteous enough. Eden satisfies this element. Much of his work was directed, admittedly without full success, to arresting the march of dictatorships. Many of his speeches are so full of righteous sentiments as to be fit for delivery as sermons. Here, then, is a considerable floating vote which Eden might net for the triumphant satisfaction of the comfortable middle classes of Britain.

Not only can he sound virtuous, he can look "nice." Today the female vote in Great Britain outnumbers that of the men by hundreds of thousands. Even though a near view of Eden is disillusioning, he looks grand in the distance. Women persist in thinking he is "lovely." This is true only by comparison with some of the other candidates for the premiership.

He cannot be called "hard-faced." His features, as I said, are a gift to a skillful photographer, instead of a desperate problem. It is hardly to be supposed that the managers of the Tory party have forgotten the qualities Eden displayed in the sales department when the League of Nations was being sold at the general election of 1935. It has been said that back-benchers would go up to him before and after the campaign saying, "You did me a lot of good in my constituency."

There is inevitably the jealousy stimulated by success in a young man, but this pill has been swallowed before.

There could not be much more resentment at his becoming prime minister in 1942 than at his having been foreign secretary in 1936. Something more than presentability is necessary to become the democratic leader of the party of power and education. Has Mr. Eden that quality which Kipling described as "essential guts"? Is he too much of a "gentleman" to trample down rivals and opponents?

Some kind of answer can be found in his language and bearing on critical occasions. It is worth while reading his speech of resignation on February 21, 1938. It was dignified and well expressed. It was free from complaint or recrimination. Germany's violent entry into Austria less than three weeks afterward makes one passage seem ominous and significant: "I should not be frank with the House if I were to pretend that it [i.e., the opening of negotiations with Italy] is an isolated issue as between the prime minister and myself. It is not. Within the last few weeks upon one most important decision of foreign policy which did not concern Italy at all the difference was fundamental."

The House of Commons buzzed momentarily with whispered speculation. Even now it is not known for certain whether Eden had Austria in mind, whether he was aware of what was coming to Vienna, and, if so, whether he wanted to take the risk of standing firm against Hitler's designs.

The last sentences of the same speech are important: "I do not believe that we can make progress in European appeasement . . . if we allow the impression to gain currency abroad that we yield to constant pressure. I am certain that progress depends above all on the temper of the nation, and that temper must find expression in a

firm spirit. That spirit, I am confident, is there. Not to
give voice to it is, I believe, fair neither to this country
nor to the world."

These sentences carry the maximum of punch. They
are adequate; they hint at much, but discreetly state little,
yet, when delivered, failed to do justice to the terrific
occasion.

Mr. Eden's lieutenant, Lord Cranborne, the undersecretary for foreign affairs, resigned with him. Cranborne is the grandson of the Victorian prime minister,
Lord Salisbury. He followed Eden with another speech
of "personal explanation." His statement was the more
powerful of the two—although until that day Cranborne
had seemed to be a far lighter piece of artillery. He had
been Eden's parliamentary private secretary and had
accompanied him to Geneva and on his various expedi-
tions to Continental capitals. When Eden was elevated
in 1935 to the novel office of "minister without portfolio
for League of Nations affairs," Cranborne became undersecretary for foreign affairs. Those who did not know his
merits busily murmured that here was an instance of
Tory nepotism at its worst—another undeserved dignity
for a member of the Cecil clan. His performances in
debate and at question time tended to justify this complaint. He would wave aside sound and fair criticism by
attempts at facetiousness, even when answering Winston
Churchill or Lloyd George.

How deceptive are these appearances! His work at
Geneva, oral and written, was masterly. And when the
test of character came he stood out in the House of
Commons with the manner of Hippocleides and the
voice of Pericles. His limbs are even less co-ordinated
than Eden's. Like many other Cecils he is round-shoul-

dered. His nose is straight and prominent and he generally seems to be smiling behind his spectacles.

Those who do not know him would say, "Here is a
fellow of a poor physique which matches a second-rate
intellect." After a few conversations, in which Cranborne
makes no attempt to play the great man, the first impres-
sions begin to be dissipated. You discover a man of play-
ful tongue but passionate sincerity of spirit.

On this occasion he stood up with a becoming assump-
tion of modesty. He explained why he agreed with Eden.
Then came the rhetorical thunderbolt. He specified the
various ways by which the Italians could give evidence
of good will: "I must confess that in default of such
evidence I am afraid that for His Majesty's government
to enter on official conversations would be regarded not
as a contribution to peace, but as a surrender to blackmail!"

This phrase embodied in a flash the contempt of the
House of Cecil for something that one of its most important representatives deemed to be moral cowardice. The
noise that followed was like a lid blowing off a saucepan.
Mr. Churchill, sitting two benches below the retiring
ministers, cheered so loudly that the scars of his motor
accident showed in deep ruts upon a purple countenance.
Some branches of the Cecil family have deprecated this
robustness of language. But why need Cranborne care?
He is doomed before so very long to take his father's
place in the Lords. Why should not the future Lord Salisbury tell the whole truth?

Cranborne, because of his lordly fate, cannot in these
days be considered as a possible prime minister—unless
Britain removes that slightly ridiculous constitutional
bar which prevents a peer from sitting or speaking in the

Commons. After his resignation he spoke quite as well as Eden. And on that February 21st he exhibited the one quality which Eden seemed to lack, the power to hit hard regardless of consequences. Could Eden have used the words "surrender to blackmail"? Eden might have been on the point of playing also the authentic spokesman of democracy. But, as the words were forming themselves, by some unhappy magic that badge of genteel inhibition, his Old Etonian tie with the thin blue stripes on the broad black ground, would administer a little tweak of warning—and the words would die away in his throat. "My dear man, you really can't say that!" This delicacy is to be deplored. Cranborne also is entitled to wear an Old Etonian tie.

More than seven months passed before Eden again spoke in the House of Commons. The Anschluss came and passed a few days after his resignation. It was too short a period for him to intervene with a gracefully worded "I told you so!" But among all who possessed knowledge or feeling the anxieties about Czechoslovakia grew and grew. The climax of the year's anguish was reached on September 30th at Munich. From Monday, October 3rd, till Friday, the 6th, the debate rolled on. Some of the scores of members of the House of Commons who wished to speak in eulogy, comment, or criticism of Neville Chamberlain were heard.

On the Monday Anthony Eden did all three before a full House. His praise and comment were direct. His criticism was oblique, and most gentlemanly. His penultimate sentence struck the note which he followed for months: "If there ever were a time for a call for a united effort by a united nation, it is my conviction that that time is now." His whole speech would repay close attention from those seeking a balanced and objective and informed presentation. It is impossible to decide whether this utterance was actuated by any deep motive, and, if so, whether it was partly personal or wholly patriotic. It reads most admirably, but that is not always the best compliment to pay a speech. Eden spoke for nearly three-quarters of an hour in the early evening before the House had begun to grow weary. His peroration roused some lukewarm applause.

The next day, for a mere fifteen minutes, at a moment when the chamber was beginning to empty for dinner, Cranborne made his contribution. He seemed pale with shame and suppressed passion. A Cecil may be expected to know the meaning of the word "honor." At once Cranborne was attacking Chamberlain's maladroit appropriation of Disraeli's phrase "peace with honor." "Peace he certainly brought back to us, and there is not one of us who will not wish to thank him with a full heart for that priceless gift . . . but where is honor? I have looked and looked but I cannot see it. It seems to me a wicked mockery to describe by so noble a name the agreement which has been reached." So he went on, sparing neither Hitler nor Chamberlain.

Once again the noble lieutenant's sentences were more telling than the speech of his former chief. When the news of the Munich terms came through, Eden may have winced at the "wicked mockery" of "peace with honor." But could he bring himself to brand Chamberlain's arrogance with such language? The answer must be "No" and the reason must be sought, for Eden is not without verbal resource.

If ever there was a propitious moment for a revolt, that moment was Munich. Austria gone, Czechoslovakia ruined, the "firm spirit" for which he had pleaded seven months before quite absent, the country bewildered and relieved, but half ashamed of its relief—such was the union of favorable conditions. Anthony could have brandished a sword, he preferred to wave the notes of a sermon. He would have been the "key man." Winston Churchill might have jumped into the saddle and become prime minister, but no revolt that did not include Eden could have hoped for success.

On what support could Eden have counted if he had chosen this moment? The dissident Conservatives, that is, those who abstained from voting in the Munich debate, would have been sure to rally to his side. Numerically they were small, but qualitatively they were not to be despised. Besides Eden and Cranborne there were Duff Cooper, Churchill, Amery, and Lord Wolmer—and about two score more, most of whom were willing to think for themselves rather than to echo automatically the verbally inspired pronouncements of the leader. Moreover, there were plenty more in the Conservative party who managed to enter the government lobby but did so in a mood of cheerless humiliation. A clearer call might have brought out more members of the Cabinet than Duff Cooper. But of that no one can as yet be certain, as Cabinet secrecy is a real thing.

Most of the Opposition Liberals would, it may be safely assumed, have switched into line behind Eden—and Churchill—for reasons of self-preservation and moral exaltation. A country which prefers the easily comprehended arangement of two parties preserves an electoral system which discourages the existence of more than one Opposition. But the total Liberal voting strength spread over the whole country is not to be despised. Most of the

Labor party would at that moment have joined in a supreme combined effort to defeat Chamberlain and his followers. For once the machine would have clanked less loudly than the call of national necessity. Eden chose to reject the opportunity. He preferred to deliver a speech of documentary excellence culminating in an appeal for "unity."

This unexceptionable plea has often been repeated in speeches in this country and in a number of articles which he found time to write for the press. Unity for what? Unity under whom? Neither what Eden said nor what he wrote has supplied an answer to these pertinent questions. He found unity under Chamberlain personally impossible, but when he urged unity without specifying an alternative leader he placed under a debt of gratitude the very prime minister whom he found it impossible to continue serving.

Could it be that he occasionally regretted his holiday from office? A rumor was spread in February, 1938, that he was unwell. It was an untruth. Six and a half years of continuous and increasingly burdensome labors may have justified a short vacation but would scarcely have warranted a first-class crisis in the government.

Was he prodded into resignation by his friend and confidant Cranborne? The undersecretary probably had greater strength of character; he certainly had the advantage of slight seniority and more complete detachment.

The supporters of Chamberlain suddenly discovered that, just before Eden resigned, he had shown great and unwonted irritability. But that condition was hardly pathological. He has a hot temper, which is usually under control but has sometimes served him well. He had shown it to Mussolini. He must have been intensely "irritated" when Chamberlain, directly he became prime minister, wrote, on his own initiative, a letter of fraternal greetings to the Italian dictator. And it must have been "irritating" to see Chamberlain, whose reputation was based on finance and local administration, taking progressively more control of the Foreign Office. No doubt each of them found the other "irritating" and uncongenial.

Mere conjectures are not convincing. A more plausible theory declares that Eden is resolved to become the leader of the Conservative party at an early date. Or circumstances might demand a coalition—that political solvent for major crises. If so, the unity he has preached will stand him in good stead. He perhaps hoped to lead the Tory party along a path of his own design. So he abstained from violent attack or even the semblance of recrimination. The blows he dealt were hardly distinguishable from affectionate caresses. He may win favor with other political figures of great influence, but he risked disappointing thousands of ordinary men and women who had regarded him as a white hope.

For with a good deal of justification he had been thought of as a willing spokesman for the oppressed. Small nations, minorities, and refugees saw in Eden the symbol of British understanding and decency.

When Eden visited the United States in the winter after his resignation he was impressed by the measures that the administration there had taken to train and occupy the large numbers of unemployed young men. When he returned to England he proposed that his own country make a more energetic assault upon the mass of wasteful idleness. Political seers at once predicted that Chamberlain could and would strengthen his administration by making Eden minister of labor.

Fortunately, that did not happen. Eden was preserved for an office where his talents would be better used. If his policy of "standing firm" had been followed it is possible that war might not have broken out in September, 1939. When war came Eden was made secretary of state for the dominions. He was not included in the War Cabinet of nine, but he was given "special access" to it. His new position thus brought him in closer touch with the empire's conduct of the war than he would have been as minister of war. Even so, in some respects the position is neither wholly suitable nor completely satisfactory.

With the exception of Winston Churchill, Anthony Eden was the only important member of the war government who entered it with mind and body refreshed. For a year and a half he had been able to write, to read, to speak as and when he liked—free. He was able to enjoy a thing precious to him, the society of his wife and of his two sons, one in his early teens, the other six years younger.

With an anxiety approaching agony he saw things go from bad to worse during the period after he had resigned from office. Retreat after retreat was thinly cloaked with the euphemism "appeasement." The Anschluss, Munich, the ides of March in 1939—this procession of disasters finally sank to the attack upon Poland and the war against Hitler to implement Britain's pledged word. He watched the headlong deterioration resulting from the muddled misreading by his former colleagues of the character of the evil governing clique in Germany.

Utterly and bitterly vindicated, but too proud to point to his vindication, he was automatically invited to return. If he is to be in office he should, on the grounds of qualifications and experience, be foreign secretary or prime minister. Instead, he is dominions secretary, an office certainly important but hardly commensurate with Eden's equipment.

Of what does the work of this office consist? To some extent it is comparable with the job of a foreign secretary. Each minister is in charge of the relations between the United Kingdom and other nations. But, whereas the sphere of the foreign secretary is the whole world, that of the dominions secretary is a limited part of the British Empire, more accurately called "the British Commonwealth of Nations."

That second title is no empty phrase. By far the larger part of what was formerly the British Empire has, since the First German War, become a commonwealth. The "colonies"—a great number of territories such as British Guiana, Malta, Ceylon, Nigeria, Cyprus, and so on—are ultimately controlled by a secretary of state for the colonies working in the Colonial Office in Whitehall. India, also, while enjoying a larger measure of self-government than is commonly appreciated, has her relationships with Britain regulated and directed by a secretary of state for India.

But Britain's greatest achievement by far in the realm of political history has resulted from the lesson taught her on the North American continent between 1776 and 1783. Her policy toward the bulk of the territories which have come within her control has been to accord them the rights of self-government at the earliest possible moment. This conduct has produced unity instead of disaffection.

In no sense does England exercise an "empire" over Canada, Newfoundland, Australia, New Zealand, or South Africa. Each country is a "dominion." Each country can, if she wishes, call herself part of the British Empire. But she is now a partner in the fullest sense. Indeed, since the First German War the United Kingdom itself has theoretically ceased to be the "mother country" and has technically become a "dominion"! Two factors alone unite the Commonwealth—the crown and the Union Jack.

Each of the daughter nations has unfettered control of her own foreign policy. Each one of them was a free and independent member state of the League of Nations. London would no longer have any power to coerce any dominion which might desire to secede from the imperial connection. Common interests, common ideals, common loyalties, and common affections have, to an extent which has to be experienced to be believed, banished the idea of secession from the field of practical politics. But if Canada, for example, were minded to leave the family, expostulation from London would not be attempted because it could achieve nothing. The governor general represents the king. He has almost as little power, but nearly as much influence.

Canada makes an independent declaration of war upon Germany. She then energetically considers how best to promote the Allied cause. In South Africa a government which desires to stay out of the conflict falls directly the war starts and is replaced by an administration under Smuts, the great lawyer-soldier-philosopher-statesman. He fought against us forty years ago. Australia enrolls tens of thousands of men and plans at once to send squadrons of aircraft and trained airmen to Europe. New Zealand leaps into the conflict to the cry of "One Flag, One King, One Cause."

John Bull invites Uncle Sam to suppress his smiles at this mild spate of boasting. Give us a little credit for being able to digest what you had to teach us at the end of the eighteenth century. And let anyone beware who refers to Canada or any other dominion as a "colony"!

One of Eden's earliest actions in his new office was to invite each dominion to send a representative to London to consult upon and to co-ordinate the war efforts of the Commonwealth. South Africa sent Colonel Reitz, who had fought against us in the South African War.

The partner nations in the British Commonwealth are entitled to expect a distinguished man to preside over the Dominions Office. They have him in Anthony Eden. He is used to resolving far knottier problems than any with which they are likely to present him. Southern Eire—the territory south of Ulster—may need the tactful treatment due to a neighboring neutral occupying a strategic position of vital importance. She will enjoy from Eden the respect she deserves. He was never the man to bicker unnecessarily with any people who are intensely conscious of their own nationhood. As unfalteringly as anyone he gives the word "Eire" its proper pronunciation—to rhyme with "Sarah" and not "fiery."

I foresee for him a smooth tenure of office, if the lot of a minister can be smooth when his country is at war. But the Dominions Office, important as it is, can hardly be regarded as much more than an interlude in his distinguished career. The probabilities of his becoming prime minister well before the end of the forties are considerable. He is young and his mind is refreshed by a longish absence from office.

If that probability is translated into fact, his wife would add to his dignity. Despite his conventional background he would present a wholly new type of premier. He has risen to be a statesman well known and greatly admired throughout England, the Commonwealth, and the world.

Yet there is still about him the charm, the glamour, and the appearance of youth. At one and the same time he is a serious overgrown boy, a friendly well-mannered youth, and a man who looks like a soldier and thinks like an artist. He is one of whom his friends are so sincerely fond that, with real tenderness, they speak of him as *"Dear Anthony!"*

CHAPTER VII

LESLIE HORE-BELISHA

Bombs and Belisha Beacons

THERE are less than half a million Jews in England—rather fewer than there were in Germany before Austria was raped. Today they are largely concentrated in our great cities. Leeds has the highest percentage—over 30,000 in a population of half a million. Manchester, a city of a million, has more than 50,000. There is also a large Jewish community in the Whitechapel district of London.

Their energies are found in most trades and professions. Agriculture alone does not seem to attract them in England. Nowhere does the Jew predominate, except perhaps among the executives of the film industry. He is active behind the scenes of our theaters—and not seldom in front of them.

The detractors of Jewry say absurd things. They say the Jews control British finance. Of the hundred directors of our five great joint-stock banks no more than three are Jews. They allege a similar Jewish influence in our press. The truth is that there is only one Jewish editor of a great London daily paper—Lord Southwood, who edits the Labor *Daily Herald*.

This point deserves emphasis. The general absence of racial and religious discrimination in Britain and the United States is one of the hallmarks of the great democ-

Leslie Hore-Belisha, until recently Secretary of State for War, with the King of England. Hore-Belisha will be remembered as the man who had ready in the autumn of 1939 an army far greater, both in actual strength and in the capacity for rapid expansion, than General French's "Contemptible Little Army" of 1914. He will be celebrated as the man who, in disregard of claims of seniority, elevated younger men to top commands in the army, and on whose shoulders fell the heavy burden of putting conscription into effect.

racies. Jews are eminent in many places. Epstein is the greatest British sculptor. There are plenty of famous Jewish musicians here. One of the biggest catering firms in Britain is Lyons. In all large centers can be found a branch of Marks & Spencer. A great tailoring business has been founded by Sir Montague Burton. And good luck to them.

The Englishman and the American do not fear the Jew. And the Jew certainly does not fear Uncle Sam or John Bull. We hope he respects us. In any event, he is a part of the nation. Jew and Gentile should be mutually grateful. The man who in my opinion was the greatest of all prime ministers was the Jew Benjamin Disraeli.

There is a sprinkling—but no more than a sprinkling— of Jews in Parliament. English public life without its successful Jews—a decent but not a dominant leaven—would be a contradiction in terms. Britain has been hitherto self-regarding enough to realize that an element of Jewish stock makes for the total strength of the body politic.

Of our Jewish community the Right Honorable Leslie Hore-Belisha, at the age of forty-six, is among the most successful. Whatever further distinctions lie ahead of him, Leslie Hore-Belisha will be remembered as the secretary of state for war who had ready in the autumn of 1939 an army far greater, both in actual strength and in the capacity for rapid expansion, than General French's "Contemptible Little Army" of 1914. He will be celebrated as the man who, in disregard of the claims of seniority, promoted Lord Gort to the position of chief of the Imperial General Staff, later to be commander in chief of the British Expeditionary Force in France. The political head of the army helping to smash the Nazis is a Jew.

These are high services for a youngish man to have rendered the realm. They indicate decisiveness, boldness, and self-confidence. Certainly Mr. Hore-Belisha has already done enough to remain an especially significant figure on the long scroll of our secretaries of state for war. But before he held that office his earlier activities had everywhere made his name a household word.

Indeed, Hore-Belisha's name has long been "news." Its owner has a certain faculty for publicizing himself. The name itself is striking, exotic to English eyes and ears. It is literally unique.

The second syllable of "Belisha" should rhyme with "me" and not "I." Clever people have suggested that the hyphen be advanced a single letter so that Mount Horeb and the prophet Elisha might be properly celebrated by a famous name. A little research will prove that there is no contemporary warranty for this attractive emendation.

Leslie was born in 1893 to Mr. and Mrs. J. I. Belisha. Five months later Leslie's father died. In 1912 his mother married a second time. Her second husband, only nineteen years older than his stepson, was Sir Adair Hore who in 1935 became permanent secretary to the Ministry of Pensions. Mr. Hore-Belisha's mother, who had thus become Lady Hore, died in 1936. He was a devoted son and felt the bereavement bitterly. That is the whole story of his name. So, as a judge might say, let us hear no more nonsense about "Horeb-Elisha."

Master Leslie was sent to school at Clifton where a number of other Jewish boys have gone. Indeed, one entire "house" is reserved for them. He was as fleet of foot as he was nimble of mind. Twice he won the hundred-yard. The war came, and when hostilities ended he had, at the age of twenty-five, reached field rank.

Major Hore-Belisha resumed his interrupted studies at

St. John's College, Oxford. "Here is a winner," said an undergraduate population consisting of schoolboys and warriors, and made him president of the Union. Hore-Belisha decided that he was a Liberal; so he was, a Liberal with a belief in empiricism, a faith in the power of the individual and a contempt for the soft cushions of Socialism.

He was called to the bar. Just off the Strand, on the boundaries of the City of London, is a congregation of lovely eighteenth century buildings known as "The Temple." Here barristers have their "chambers"—rooms which correspond with the "offices" of the less dramatic branch of the legal profession known as solicitors. The Temple is situated near Fleet Street, the eastern extension of the even more famous thoroughfare that runs parallel to the Thames and so is known as "The Strand." Fleet Street is the center of the London newspaper world. To the young lawyer journalism formed a physically and psychologically convenient medium of publicity.

During this period he made a number of valuable contacts. These were not transitory. Of all British politicians he has least ground for complaining that the press has ignored him or his exploits.

Although he did not win his fight in 1922 he did astonishingly well; he was a good second to the sitting Conservative member. In 1923 every circumstance conspired to help him. The Liberal rupture between Lloyd George and Asquith was healed—temporarily as it turned out, but adequately for his immediate purpose. He could fight under the joint leadership of two former prime ministers.

Lloyd George saw and appreciated his worth and so Leslie has never had to endure the shafts of that most formidable of critics. Even though Leslie Hore-Belisha has strayed from the fold that they once inhabited together, Mr. Lloyd George cannot withhold his satisfaction at the progress of the young man he helped to discover.

During his first contest Hore-Belisha took advantage of a mistake his Conservative opponent was alleged to have made. Leslie charged him with having said that he was too young to sit in Parliament, that he was "a little chit of a fellow." If such a stricture was ever made it was most indiscreet, for it gave Hore-Belisha the kind of opportunity on which he thrives.

Leslie was twenty-nine, so he compared himself with a series of great historical figures who had done tremendous deeds at an early age. He fashioned a purple passage in which he said he was "older than Pitt when he became the first minister of the crown, a little younger than Wolfe when he scaled the Heights of Abraham." Thrills and applause animated the audience of the young spellbinder. He repeated this patch of eloquence whenever and wherever an opportunity arose.

Hore-Belisha maintained this level of rhetoric the next time, and won. By a substantial majority for 1923, when the electorate was much smaller than today and margins were habitually more narrow, "the major" was elected. Since that date he has taken good care to strengthen his local grip. Devonport has enjoyed being represented by a man who, whatever else may be said about him, cannot be dismissed as a nonentity.

He early learned every trick of the politicians' trade—how to greet, how to accept congratulations, to whom to be deferential, when to conciliate, when to hit, above all—though he was merely perfecting an instrument already acute—how to debate. He suffered neither from diffidence nor from false modesty.

Within the Liberal party he made his presence felt. His survival of his party's crash at the election of 1924 gave him the immense advantage of uninterrupted experience in Parliament. On that occasion his majority fell to a mere half thousand. In 1929 it swelled to nearly five thousand. At the last two elections he has polled more than two to one. In this particular instance personality—so widely blazoned by publicity—has certainly counted electorally. But Hore-Belisha has something more. He has always had an uncanny perception of what his public wants.

He is happy in politics, and happiness facilitates industry. "Handy with his tongue," as he has been epigrammatically described, he has not relied on the spur of the moment when the course of the skirmish could be foreseen. He has been known to work for hours to prepare the best possible presentation of an apparently trivial point.

Until 1931 Hore-Belisha enjoyed the exhilaration of continuous opposition. When the Tories were in power he could speak as a Liberal. During the two periods of Labor administration, still as a Liberal, he could play the gadfly and sting the second-rate Socialist ministers. His wit and ingenious insolence became famous. He was not even beyond bickering with some of the senior members of his own party. During the whole of this rollicking period he remained the smart-tongued, intellectually adolescent president of the Oxford Union.

By 1931 he had eight years' parliamentary experience behind him. He saw in the collapse of Labor the great opportunity. He acted as a kind of messenger between the most prominent among the severest Liberal critics of the government and the other political heads. His friends in

Fleet Street were careful to make known the part he had taken in the formation of the National government.

And now his brains were to be rewarded, his ambition was to be at least pleasantly whetted. After the election he was given an office where his Liberal career would be useful during the retreat from free imports. He was made parliamentary secretary to the Board of Trade while Mr. Walter Runciman, another "Liberal National," became president.

At once Hore-Belisha showed a Churchillian ability to make any office with which he was associated assume an importance not necessarily proportionate to its true significance. He could now choose his ground more profitably than ever, so he redoubled the diligence he bestowed on his parliamentary preparations.

One of his targets was now the section of Opposition Liberals who still believed in the historic principle of free trade. Once, when replying to a debate on our trade position, he tricked out statistics in a most attractive manner, pointed to the benefits which tariffs were yielding, and concluded his argument by bringing his fist down on the box and declaring "an ounce of practice is worth a ton of principle!" In this single phrase Hore-Belisha condensed his own political philosophy.

He was too good for this subordinate job. Within twelve months the same Ramsay MacDonald whom he had badgered so satirically promoted him to be financial secretary to the Treasury, bringing him to the threshold of the Cabinet. In this office his new chief was Neville Chamberlain, the chancellor of the exchequer; his work could be observed at the closest range by the most powerful individual next to Stanley Baldwin.

The period during which he achieved the zenith of his

notoriety—Belisha's golden age—began in June, 1934, when he was put in charge of the Ministry of Transport. His idea for reducing road accidents was to install on the highways the "Hore-Belisha beacons"—uprights seven or eight feet tall painted black and white, not unlike barbers' poles, and surmounted by balls of a lurid orange hue. In populous areas they mark the crossings where pedestrians have right of way over road traffic. Like the man who introduced them, they are too conspicuous to be missed. No one can say with certainty, however, whether these peculiar emblems reduced the great and growing number of fatalities.

They and other simultaneous regulations certainly did one thing which can hardly have failed to gratify the new minister of transport. However little he may have done to conceive the idea, the Belisha beacons made the name of the new Disraeli familiar in every household in Great Britain. Had his predecessor, Oliver Stanley, the second son of Lord Derby, been transferred to the Ministry of Labor a few weeks later, the Belisha beacons would probably have had to be content with the less outlandish title of "Stanley standard."

The post of minister of transport grew in prestige and Leslie grew with it. Mr. Baldwin, moved by his work and his wit, promoted him to the Cabinet in October, 1936. In May, 1937, Neville Chamberlain appointed him secretary of state for war.

After solving a multitude of fresh problems he began to rearrange our military furniture. New methods of attracting recruits were evolved. Life in the army was made more attractive, the soldiers' pay was raised, and the medical tests on enlistment were made less pedantic and more realistic. Promotion from the ranks was facilitated.

Major Hore-Belisha was to show his supreme authority in more serious ways. He shook up the General Staff, removing some officers and promoting others. To some men he gave notice as summarily as it was sudden. Lord Gort's standing and proved bravery fascinated the major, who made him chief of the Imperial General Staff.

In the First German War Viscount Gort had been a colonel in the Guards. He won the rarely awarded Victoria Cross for an act of great devotion and daring. Though severely wounded and in great danger he had continued to direct an attack which was in the end successful. The British Army is under the supreme orders of the French General Gamelin. But Gamelin will find it difficult to ask it to do anything which its own commander would not himself dare to do.

Belisha was sent on a courtesy visit to Italy. It was whispered that for Britain to send a Jew to Mussolini was a delicate method of mortifying Hitler. But this visit did not discourage the Duce from persisting in his attack on republican Spain or from officially introducing anti-Semitism at a later date. To Hore-Belisha, when he got home, fell the task of explaining away the batteries that were said to be menacing the bastion of Gibraltar. He did not seem to relish this task, for his smile was noticeably more apologetic and expansive than usual.

But this passing problem—or what he no doubt wanted to treat as a passing problem—was quite insignificant beside his part during the summer of 1938 in the controversy about our alleged deficiency in protection against air attack. The secretary of state for war may have contributed to the storm by his zeal for his own authority. His interesting personality here suffered its first jolt. Until the various inquiries began, Belisha's ill-wishers were strenuously discussing the possibility of his resignation and the rising statesman began to fear for his neck. But he lived through an anxious period, and so came to present the army estimates for 1939.

For the first time since November, 1918, the House heard that in certain circumstances we were to be committed to sending an expeditionary force abroad. Winston Churchill described this policy as part of the bill we are paying for Munich. The Territorial Army was increased and then doubled. We scattered guarantees over Eastern Europe. By the end of April, Chamberlain announced the introduction of compulsory military service. Upon Hore-Belisha fell the main departmental burden.

When Hore-Belisha introduced the army estimates in the spring of 1938 Britain was preparing out of her strategic reserve five divisions. Not one of them was upon a Continental scale. The European sky darkened deeply and rapidly. In March of 1939 the five were increased to nineteen, all upon a Continental scale; in April the divisions were increased to thirty-two.

The dispatch to France of the earliest units of the British Expeditionary Force in the first five weeks of the present war was a superb achievement for which credit must be assigned to the man who organized it. Hore-Belisha presided over a small body of selected officers with no more than seven confidential clerks and typists.

Every detail of the plan for transporting to France part of the army and the Royal Air Force was worked out in secret. Even the minutest needs were provided for. As a precaution against possible air attacks by the Germans, the army and its machines followed devious routes to the ports of embarkation. They went in small groups, and moved by night. By day they halted in concealment. Thus, well within forty days 158,000 men had been transported to France. There was not a single casualty.

On an average three convoys crossed the water in the darkness of each night. Besides the soldiers more than 25,000 vehicles were conveyed to France. Some of these were vast machines including tanks weighing fifteen tons apiece. In the modern British Army each battalion has, along with other weapons, fifty Bren guns and twenty-two antitank rifle~

Moreover, the British garrisons in the Middle East and elsewhere were, during those opening weeks, powerfully reinforced. Part of the British Army, the antiaircraft units, remain in Britain awaiting the marauders of the air. Twelve months after the controversy about our ground defense Belisha is confident that all is as well as it can possibly be.

But every day more men, guns, vehicles, stores, and munitions have gone on pouring into France to help to man the western front. Today there is at Britain's command an army of at least one million. As long as the war lasts its size will grow and grow. The amateur experiments of 1914 cannot be repeated. Hore-Belisha has given a professional appearance to the enterprise of 1939.

This captivating record of private enterprise and public service compels an admiration for the intelligence of the British secretary of state for war. He has done all in his power to "get on." He has made a study of the whole public and of the several diverse sections of it whose favor he has to woo.

He knows the House of Commons will appreciate cleverness if it is sustained by industry and knowledge. Accordingly, as a parliamentarian, he will be clever after diligently amassing the necessary facts.

He is aware that woolliness is fatal, so he argues deliberately in a clear if slightly rasping voice. He seems to have thought out in advance the pitch and emphasis most suitable for every sentence. In the House he is sparing of rhetoric, but not on the platform.

Though he is still nominally a Liberal, Hore-Belisha is supposed to be modeling himself after Disraeli. However, for Hore-Belisha there was no dismal or ludicrous anticlimax to any extravagantly ambitious first attempt to storm Westminster. He has found other ways of self-advertisement than Oriental curls and prodigality of attire.

The elimination of alternatives has made many Conservatives toy with the notion of his becoming their leader. But almost as many others do not forget that he was not always the loyal henchman of a Conservative prime minister and many of his earliest sallies were directed against the things for which they stand.

At times, Hore-Belisha has been criticized for the inability to swallow wholesale every decision of his colleagues. The House of Commons was recently asked to ratify a policy for Palestine by which the Arabs should after five years be able to decide whether any more Jews could immigrate into their own national home! Hore-Belisha was absent from the vote.

One would have thought it unnecessary for the press to treat this mild and passive resistance as a breach of Cabinet discipline. Would these critics have admired him more if he had positively supported what no Jew could possibly acclaim? The security of his own position did not cause him to forget the tribulations of others.

But these evidences of feeling have been sought for somewhat arduously in Mr. Hore-Belisha. He is a bachelor—married to politics. The dominant impression he makes is of a man astute to the point of hardness, to whom politics is a pursuit to be followed with all his heart and all his mind. To him politics is a deadly serious game, fit only for the professional. He is a master of detail and is afraid that a detail may paralyze a movement.

When the Liberals who followed Simon became junior partners in the National government he was deeply concerned over the choice of an attractive name. "Liberal National" may well be his own invention. And assuredly it is worth a great deal in the country.

Any Liberal National candidate can claim the total available Conservative support as well as that of all who are attracted by the word "Liberal." After election such "Liberal Nationals" will probably never offend their Conservative allies by word or vote. There are still tens of thousands among the electorate who are unaware that in practice there is not an ounce of difference between Liberal National and unqualified Conservative.

Being a Liberal National is an aid to attainment of office. In a Cabinet of twenty-three there are two right honorable gentlemen who are called "National Labor" and no less than five Liberal Nationals. But when the moment comes for the selection of a "National" leader antecedents and tradition will become mountainous obstacles.

Some Conservatives think it would be a convenient arrangement for themselves and for him if Hore-Belisha were to lead them to a number of resounding triumphs in Parliament and in the constituencies. They should approach him with the humble petition and advice that he should forthwith become in name what many say he already is in fact—a good Conservative. If he delays making this move for much longer he may find the public reaction in Britain less sympathetic than today.

Meanwhile, before they can follow him as their leader, his distinguished audiences may admire him as their spokesman. And Leslie Hore-Belisha, who is still three parts playboy, will, as he brings the House down with his more victorious performances, smile in remotely self-conscious delight. Then he will take care to drop his eyes with pity for his victim and with the modest humility of the well-bred.

PUBLISHER'S NOTE—*The resignation of Leslie Hore-Belisha as Secretary of War was announced on January 5th just as this book was going to press. Nevertheless, it is doubtful if so vigorous and original a personality as Leslie Hore-Belisha will remain in the obscurity of the back benches of Parliament for long.*

Mr. Hore-Belisha's successor in office is Oliver Stanley, whose father, the Earl of Derby, was Secretary of War from 1916 to 1918 and from 1922 to 1924. Though not a well-known or popular figure, Oliver Stanley has been long associated with public affairs and he headed the Board of Trade when the Anglo-American trade treaty was signed. A member of one of the richest and most powerful families in England, Oliver Stanley's new position confirms the remark of one political observer that "England always fights wars with a Stanley at the War Office at least part of the time."

CHAPTER VIII

DUFF COOPER

Baldwin's Young Man

THE subject of this chapter is peculiar among the nine personalities described in this book. As I write, he is not a member of the government. But I believe I shall show that he deserves to be included among men who are wielding power. He is barely fifty, and it is my belief that, though he has held high office, the more impressive part of his career is yet to come.

At a time when an unqualified devotion to France was suspect in most quarters, Sir Austen Chamberlain proclaimed that he loved her like a woman. Similarly, one of the governing emotions of Duff Cooper has been an intense affection for the sister democracy across the Channel, combined with a profound mistrust of Germany. Remember that, and his outlook will be clear. From his lips you will seldom hear the conventional discrimination between the German rulers and the German people. That distinction persists in the minds of many good-natured English people, though they are at war with a German people that either tolerates or adores Nazidom.

Duff Cooper cannot avoid taking sides in the secular antagonism between Teuton and Gaul. He stands with the Gaul. To him the present German regime is simply a manifestation of a brutish and brutal facet of the German character. That Germany repels him does no credit to the Germans. His respect is a thing worth having, for though falsely estimated a lightweight, he is a highly accomplished man.

As he has progressed in responsibility and passed through ever-sharpening crises he has developed significantly. Neither in behavior nor in appearance is he the Duff Cooper of ten years ago. Today he is someone to reckon with. Till recently he was treated as a promising but indiscreet young politician. But a turning point has come in his life: the days of promise and oral unsteadiness are over. He is steady, sober, responsible, but still brilliant.

Possibly his physique formed the impression of callowness. He had the look of a young soldier, almost a drummerboy, who lived to beat the summons to attention. Perhaps he has had more leisure in his recent retirement, for he is now acquiring the outlines of middle age and his manner has mellowed with his tongue. The drummerboy has given place to the comfortable field officer.

Henceforth Duff Cooper's corporeal expansion will neutralize his apparent lack of inches. Gentleness has been invading this brisk young spirit. The fact is that he is changing physically and spiritually before the eyes of the men and women among whom he moves. At this very moment his mind is stepping finally out of the lush garden of youth onto the hard highroad of responsibility. Given reasonable health, Duff Cooper is going to matter considerably in the days to come.

Before he entered Parliament he had behind him Eton, New College, Oxford, and a gallant career in the army as an officer in the Grenadier Guards. When he was admitted to the Distinguished Service Order he really had performed distinguished service. Nobody could call him a coward or a fool. Fortune united him with a woman of envied and classical loveliness, whose portraits, when she was Lady Diana Manners, had packed the illustrated social weeklies. Photographs, paintings, and sketches of this exquisite daughter of the Duke of Rutland were nailed to walls of dugouts in France, during the First German War.

For ten years Duff Cooper served in the Foreign Office and so was confirmed in his tilt toward France. The men with the power of final decision are the Cabinet, and the foreign secretary in particular. But for many years the counsel of their expert advisers in the Foreign Office has been: "Keep close to France. Have patience with her anxieties. Is she not next door to the danger? Has she not been invaded twice within living memory? If Britain loses French friendship she will face ruin." And who dares to say they have been wrong?

Aged thirty-four, but looking younger, this trim Guards officer entered the House in 1924, for the constituency of Oldham. Oldham is one of the many grim towns in the industrial belt of Lancashire. The volume of smoke rising from its forest of chimneys is an index of the prosperity of the cotton trade. Indifference to the claims of "local men" has seldom produced so strange a result as Duff Cooper's fleeting representation of that center of clogs, cobbled streets, and belching chimneys.

In the House he delivered a maiden speech so bright that it impressed those who imagined that English society produces only nitwits. The *Daily Mail*, a paper which later treated him with less respect, published a photograph in which Duff Cooper looked like a military angel. He was on the wing.

Within four years he actually reached the ranks of the

Duff Cooper, "till recently treated as a promising but indiscreet politician," is today "steady, sober, responsible but still brilliant." From the beginning he, probably more than any one person in the English political scene, has had a profound mistrust of Germany.

government, for he impressed Baldwin sufficiently to make him financial secretary to the War Office. He would have to act as the political lieutenant of the head of the army—the secretary of state for war.

Oldham was too near the margin to keep him when the Labor tide ran high in 1929. Only a less obviously "upper class" candidate, a more assiduous cultivator of the wayward affections of the Industrial North would have had the remotest chance of withstanding the flood.

So acceptable, however, was the Duff Cooper of those days to the ruling Tory personalities that he was soon nominated for the romantic division of Winchester. This is a "safe" Conservative seat; seldom has it returned to Parliament a member of another party. It has many features which foster Conservatism. There is no great indus-:ry to breed Socialism among trade-unionists. There is no export trade to encourage a free trade Liberal candidate. The cathedral there is a superb monument of Norman architecture. It even rivals in majesty the Grand Central Station in New York. At Winchester is a "public" school whose fame can rival, and in some respects outshine, that Eton which bred Duff Cooper. Its intimate charm is as lovely as the grandeur of the incomparable cathedral.

The young ex-minister could confidently expect a serene return to the House at an early general election. But his victorious re-entry was advanced some months by the blundering tactics of Lords Rothermere and Beaverbrook. These gentlemen were ennobled by Lloyd George at the end of the First German War. They are vulgarly known as the "press barons." Each owns a number of newspapers, Rothermere being identified most closely with the *Daily Mail* and Beaverbrook with the *Daily Express*. The section of the British press which they own has a daily and weekly circulation of many millions.

At the beginning of 1931 Baldwin, then leading the Conservative Opposition to MacDonald's second Labor government, was the quarry of a violent man hunt conducted in the columns of these nominally Conservative papers, the *Daily Express* and the *Daily Mail*. A number of other publications belonging to the same pair of noble lords were instructed to join in the chase. Baldwin had incurred the displeasure of these two press peers, who considered themselves immensely powerful. Not only was he charged with betraying the British rule in India—that was Lord Rothermere's special preserve—but he was actively offending Lord Beaverbrook by his passive disregard of the policy of "empire free trade." By this paradoxical slogan Lord Beaverbrook apparently meant the encirclement of the British Commonwealth with a high ring-fence of tariffs—and confound the foreigner!

Through the death of its sitting member, the St. George's Division of Westminster in London unexpectedly needed a new representative in March. As a standard-bearer of free trade within the empire Lord Beaverbrook arranged to run at the by-election one Sir Ernest Petter. This act was a direct challenge to the Conservative leadership in a Conservative stronghold and Baldwin had to accept it. Normally a book of this kind should not be troubled with detailed descriptions of by-elections. But this one proved for Duff Cooper, for Baldwin, and for British public life a turning point. For those who enjoy "rough stuff" it was also a particularly exciting episode.

Duff Cooper, who could be trusted to fight like a cornered animal, stood as a follower of the official Conservative leader. There opened one of the most unpleasant by-elections which has ever blotted even our variegated English democratic record. For violence of language and perversity of appeal it has seldom been equaled. The issue developed as a conflict between the traditional methods of appointing party leaders and the "dictatorship of the press."

Within a few days, and no doubt to his personal embarrassment, Sir Ernest Petter, an obscure but wellmeaning individual, found himself eulogized by the most driveling puffs in the press that was running him. Duff Cooper, on the other hand, suffered what he had to expect—every kind of abuse.

Most of the enemy's weapons he found himself able to parry with ease. For example, because of his declarations in favor of international co-operation he was amiably described as a "softy"; the answer necessary was to republish the notice gazetting the award of the Distinguished Service Order in France.

Less easy, and possibly less necessary, to meet was the unearthing by a newspaper office of an occasion when he had delivered in Germany a lecture entitled "An Apology for the British Empire." The imperialists of the constituency were expected to be ignorant that "apology" properly means a "reasoned explanation" and not a "shamefaced admission of guilt."

Since the campaign was proceeding during the height of the Indian controversy, the *Daily Mail* came out with headings and placards "Gandhi is watching St. George's." And Sir Ernest Petter's supporters trundled round a halfnaked life-sized effigy of the Indian leader to illustrate this slogan.

In fighting the two hostile press peers Duff Cooper de-

veloped an unsuspected flair for invective. When Beaverbrook seemed to be casting about upon Duff Cooper's
personal courage he retorted by saying in one of his
speeches, "Lord Beaverbrook has not got the guts of a
louse." This was rough language for one whose taste ran
more naturally to such things as the writing of a classic
biography of the French statesman, Talleyrand.

But this campaign was no scholar's job; he went down
in the fighting pit. He would blow himself out like a
frog and explode with vehemence before an audience
containing a big proportion of imported hecklers and
persons who had come from other parts of London to
see and share the fun. In the front row sat his elegant
wife and other celebrated relatives.

Sense was discernible amid all this ranting. When complaining that Lord Beaverbrook was trying to impose a
protectionist program on Baldwin, "This," he shouted
"is the *very policy* for which Mr. Baldwin was attacked
from the same quarter at the general election of 1923!"

Duff Cooper was irascible at question time, like many
another harassed candidate. He would mutter to his companions at the table which formed the only trace of a
"platform" in the schoolrooms where the majority of the
meetings were held, "I can't hear what the fellah is saying," or "What can the fellah mean?" He was not yet
sufficiently steeled by electioneering to know that a hot
tongue should never be suffered to interfere with a cool
head.

Yet the rough-and-tumble of the campaign did not
make him abandon all extrapolitical activities. At the
time he was broadcasting a series of critical talks on modern literature. He arrived in the studio out of breath
and some moments late. He explained his unpunctuality

in these rather unconventional words: "Some of you—puff—may know—puff—that I am engaged—puff—in a by-election." No doubt a goodly number of voters were thus reminded of his interest in their welfare.

Baldwin did not desert his young champion. In his letter of commendation he recalled that Duff Cooper was leaving a safe seat to engage in a difficult struggle. If Duff Cooper were defeated he himself might have to resign from the party leadership, so Baldwin stirred himself to what he could always do when he had his back to the wall—return the blows of his adversaries with interest. He even equaled and excelled the robust language of the candidate. If that were possible, he gave Duff Cooper a lesson in invective. At a celebrated meeting in one of London's greatest halls, Baldwin accused the press peers of wanting "power without responsibility, the prerogative of the harlot through the ages."

The attempt to govern parties and Parliament from Fleet Street was beaten. Without a good and positive candidate to carry his banner Baldwin might have lost the day.

The scenes at the declaration were in some respects reminiscent of the Eatanswill of Charles Dickens. The crowd was dense and surging, part of it noisy, part of it anxious. A collection of young toughs stood beneath the building chanting this beautiful refrain, "P-E-T-T-E-R! We want Petter!" In the crowd before the main door was a tipsy little clerk who combatively repeated again and again this pertinent question, "Who is Lord Beaverbrook, anyway?"

When the result was announced Lady Diana so far departed from her statuesque dignity as to wave the blue party colors. Howls and cheers arose before the victor himself could be heard from an upper window. When he did speak his words surprised those who had been admiring him in other and more tempestuous moods: "Let there be an end to these unhappy differences. Let us go forward from today as an united party."

Instead of representing Winchester, the ancient capital of England, Duff Cooper now found himself sitting for a fraction of modern London, situated at the back door of the Houses of Parliament, where the only opposition to official Conservatism which could raise its head was heterodox Toryism. This particular heterodoxy had been blown along by an unsavory breath and Duff Cooper found himself being treated for a time as the living expression of political decency.

He had been the center of a first-class episode. The English stunt press had been put severely in its proper place. The public recognized its right to purvey news and to distill opinion, but would have none of its attempts to dictate party loyalties or appoint party leaders.

In the summer of 1931 all seemed arranged for Duff Cooper's steady and uninterrupted progress to the highest places. He went back to his old post of financial secretary at the War Office, but this time he had the chance to shine, for the secretary of state, Lord Hailsham, was in the House of Lords. So upon Duff Cooper on three occasions fell the duty of presenting the army estimates in the House of Commons. This he did without reading a single note—to the admiration of all who were present, from his wife in the gallery to his colleagues beside him.

In midsummer of 1934 he was promoted to financial secretary to the Treasury. That office is commonly regarded as the final steppingstone before the Cabinet. This move brought him into intimate contact with

Neville Chamberlain, who was chancellor of the exchequer. For Chamberlain's judgment on matters even more important than finance Duff Cooper was later to conceive a disdain. But for this period, as far as can be ascertained, he worked harmoniously with Neville Chamberlain. Perhaps he was mildly amused if he saw his chief casting an appraising eye abroad upon the darkening scene. Neither could have foreseen the frightful climax: the personal triumph of the one at Munich and the historic vindication of the other through the war which Munich did not avoid.

After the election of 1935 Baldwin brought Duff Cooper into the executive. He became secretary of state for war and so political chief of that British Army in which he had once been a gallant officer. It was the moment of Mussolini's aggression upon Ethiopia. Duff Cooper, a believer in international order, who saw the security of the British Empire jeopardized by unchecked aggression in any quarter, spoke out at the very first Cabinet he attended in favor of the strongest possible measures against Italy.

He had a fine personal record of war service. Of him it could not be said that he was anxious to fight to the last drop of the blood of other men. He spoke as one who, knowing war, believed in peace. He foresaw the course to which affairs were drifting and took upon himself the role of alarmist. Once, when appealing for recruits, he said it was his duty "to frighten people out of their skins."

To some his language seemed mere panic-mongering. He incurred plenty of devout reprobation by attacking pacifist bishops.

The way his mind was now working could be inferred from a speech he made in Paris stressing the unity of interest between Britain and France and the reality of their "alliance." He had to try to indicate the dangerous and delusive depths by pointing to the roadstead. But for this speech the Liberal and Labor Opposition roasted him in the House. Were we returning, they asked, to the discredited principle of the balance of power?

The alleged offender sat on the Front Bench in angry silence while his conduct was subjected to a searching and hostile analysis. So cruel are the restraints placed on the tongues of ministers, and of all men Duff Cooper must suffer most when he cannot speak out. The debate was distinguished by an intervention by Winston Churchill, who liked Duff Cooper and what he had said.

When Chamberlain succeeded Baldwin as prime minister he transferred Duff Cooper from the War Office to the Admiralty. That was another step up, as the navy is both in seniority and in importance the first of the British fighting services. He moved capably through his new and august environment. When he severed himself from office sixteen months later the slanderous whisper crept around that the move was a good riddance, that he had not been an efficient first lord. This rumor was as inaccurate as it was artificial and unchivalrous. He was one of the best departmental ministers. He has grasp, application, and the faculty for harmonious relations with his staff. This is not the precise point at which to assess his judgment over the Munich settlement. But when his departure came it meant for the government a diminution of total administrative ability.

Resignations on the initiative of the retiring minister seldom come about as a result of some isolated dramatic reason. Duff Cooper, one may safely conclude, like Eden before him, endured to the limit the pursuit of a policy for which his distrust grew daily. His speech of resignation shows how near he came to lingering on a little longer. It was only the difference between Munich and Berchtesgaden that finally brought him to his momentous decision. It was "the last straw."

Here is how on October 3, 1938, Duff Cooper described the conflict in his mind:

"The prime minister will shortly be explaining to this House the particulars in which the Munich terms differ from the Godesberg ultimatum. There are great and important differences and it is a great triumph for the prime minister that he was able to acquire them. I spent the greater part of Friday [September 30th] trying to persuade myself that those terms were good enough for me. I tried to swallow them—I did not want to do what I have done—but *they stuck in my throat* because . . . there still remained the fact that Czechoslovakia was to be invaded, and I thought that after accepting the humiliation of partition *she should have been spared the ignominy and the horror of invasion.*"

Perhaps the enforced swallowing of other incidents had already given him a pain in the throat. Since July, 1936, the Spanish Civil War had been running its bloody course. Britain and France, to limit the quarrel to the boundaries of Spain and to try to avert a wider catastrophe, had proposed the policy of "nonintervention." It worked imperfectly. Munitions flowed in. Eden contended that a leaky dam was better than no dam at all. But some hateful things happened.

Duff Cooper can hardly have enjoyed the experience of having to defend the inactivity of British sailors as they witnessed from their warships the cries and struggles of the drowning in Spanish territorial waters. Any other course, he had to argue, would have meant a departure from "our great policy of nonintervention." If we had intervened to save the wretches within sight of the shore of the Basque country, should we not have been called upon to take refugees from the beach? And when our rescue party had gone so far what was to prevent them from carrying their humane expedition inland, and so on as far as Madrid? Duff Cooper was annoyed, and perhaps grieved and alarmed by the ultimate victory of the dictators in Spain.

In choosing to resign over Munich, he selected a more dramatic moment than that chosen by his friend Anthony Eden for his own exit. His "personal statement" on his resignation was a model for this important type of speech. It was, moreover, delivered at a pivotal tactical moment, Monday, October 3rd.

On the Wednesday before the prime minister had been the center of a scene which today seems to constitute the zenith of frustrated hopes. He had had his exuberant commission to go to Munich and felt that he must bring back some kind of peace. He came back amid the wildly renewed cheering of that part of the public who imagined that terms did not matter beside that chance of living which they thought threatened.

The solitary discordant public note was struck on the Saturday by Duff Cooper, when he resigned. The note was in fact a prophetic knell of danger ahead. Duff Cooper was the pioneer along the nation's way back from hysteria to reason. With the news of his sacrifice of office people were obliged to allow thought to stand up to sentiment.

But in the House his party were anxious to celebrate the alleged triumphs of their leader. They were impatient to start the cheering. Yet there was Duff Cooper with the right, as a retiring minister, to make the first speech before the start of the debate proper. Nineteen men out of twenty would have fallen short of their opportunity. They would have erred on the side of recrimination, claptrap, or self-pity.

Duff Cooper avoided all these extremes and quietly but firmly began the torpedo attack on the Chamberlain armada. The Chamberlainites were a huge majority that day, but he proceeded to deliver a perfect exposure of the flaws of Munich. So significant was this speech, so revealing of the speaker's convictions, so absolutely vindicated by the terrible march of later events that it must be sketched in outline.

His manner was impressive. Gone was the faintest trace of his earlier ranting. He appeared tired, sad, and careworn. There was no immoderate emphasis, no stormy bulging of the cheeks, no raising of the voice. He spoke as spontaneously as he had ever done. Only once in that forty minutes of acute trial did he falter and then from his waistcoat pocket he drew a piece of paper which, unfolded, could not have exceeded nine square inches. He caught up the thread, back went the "notes," and on went Duff Cooper.

The language he used was simple. He described his sense of loneliness, "when in the Cabinet room all his other colleagues were able to present him with bouquets, and it was an extremely painful and bitter moment for me that all I could offer the prime minister was my resignation." We should, he contended, always make plain exactly where we stood in an international crisis. In 1914 the Berlin crowd had smashed all the windows of the British Embassy. The members of the embassy staff had had great sympathy with them, for the German government had assured them that we should remain neutral. So now during the summer Hitler had been constantly reassured that Britain would not fight. When Duff Cooper had returned from traveling in the Scandinavian peninsula and the Baltic States at the end of August it was clear that Germany could only be prevented from going to war at the end of September by Great Britain stating that she would be in that war and on the other side.

He said that after the rape of Austria he had urged a firm declaration, but had been met with the retort that the British were not prepared to fight for Czechoslovakia. But we should have been fighting as in 1914 "in order that one great power should not be allowed, in disregard of treaty obligations, of the laws of nations, and the decrees of morality, to dominate by brutal force the continent of Europe. For that principle we fought against Napoleon Bonaparte, and against Louis XIV of France and Philip II of Spain. For that principle we must ever be prepared to fight, for on the day when we are not prepared to fight for it we forfeit our empire, our liberties, and our independence."

The guarded statements made by the prime minister and repeated by Simon were not, according to Duff Cooper's argument, the language which the dictators understood. Those dictators had introduced a new vocabulary, and talked the new language of the headlines of the tabloid press. We were always told we must not irritate Hitler: "It seems to me that Herr Hitler never makes a speech save under the influence of considerable irritation, and the addition of one more irritant would not, I should have thought, have made a great difference."

According to Duff Cooper, the prime minister lost several opportunities of making the position plain to

Hitler. He made his last appeal on the morning of Wednesday, September 28th. For the first time Hitler was prepared to yield an inch. "But I would remind the House," said the former first lord with rising drama, "that the message from the prime minister was not the first news that he [Hitler] had received that morning. *At dawn he had learned of the mobilization of the British Fleet!*" Duff Cooper claimed that he had long been urging this mobilization. It was the only language to which Hitler would pay attention—the language of the mailed fist.

He described the headlong deterioration during the time that Chamberlain had tried to move Hitler by the language of sweet reasonableness. And after all Czechoslovakia was to be invaded. *"The German government, having got their man down, were not to be deprived of the pleasure of kicking him . . . and the army was not to be robbed of its loot."* He criticized the joint declaration by Chamberlain and Hitler and then turned his attention to the new commitment we had undertaken of guaranteeing the residue of Czechoslovakia: "We have taken away the defenses of Czechoslovakia in the same breath as we have guaranteed them *as though you were to deal a man a mortal blow and at the same time insure his life."*

This new guarantee, Duff Cooper argued, should mean a great acceleration of British rearmament. We needed an army on a Continental basis. But how could we justify to the people that extra burden if, in the words of the prime minister, Munich meant "peace in our time"? The prime minister believed Hitler although he had broken the long series of engagements which Duff Cooper enumerated.

The prime minister believed that Hitler was interested only in Germany: "Well, there are Germans in other countries—in Switzerland, in Denmark and in Alsace; I think that one of the only countries in Europe in which there are no Germans is Spain, and yet there are rumors that Germany has taken an interest in that country!" Finally, as to colonies, about which Hitler had said there was no question of war; did that mean that Hitler would take "No" for an answer? Or did he believe that he would secure them "without fighting, by *well-timed bluff, bluster and blackmail*"?

There was more in this speech of a personal character. It might have been improved if he had refrained from apprehending in his final sentences the ruin of his own political career. If he in fact incurred this disaster he might perhaps be compensated by the reflection that he had secured his place in history.

For daring, for presentation, for accuracy of prognosis, this speech could not have been surpassed. If ever a man is entitled to say in public, "I told you so," that man is Duff Cooper. But outspoken as he is, his manners would never allow him so to debase Eton, Oxford, and the Guards. When Mr. Chamberlain spoke immediately afterward he made no attempt to traverse what Duff Cooper had said. He expressed the desire to make the speech he would have made if the first lord had not resigned!

These excerpts from Duff Cooper's speech have been given because they proclaim the man as he now is after many years of half-maturity. The speaker is a rare type who could hardly have been nurtured outside England. In middle age he is intellectually as brave as, when a young man, he was physically fearless. He is forthright, determined, but slightly too cocksure. He is liberal in the sense in which all educated Englishmen are liberal. He is conservative in the sense of desiring the lasting security of the British Empire. He believes in toleration, democracy, and liberty of opinion.

But Duff Cooper's ordinary conduct is not "democratic" as the word is commonly understood. He is too intellectual to be a ready companion. Indeed, most men would call him "high-brow." His society is for ordinary men an alarming and not an inspiring experience. Read his biography of Talleyrand and you will feel yourself in the company of a professor of history with a deft literary touch and a natural revulsion from the threadbare phrase. It may not be easy reading, but it is an undeniably distinguished piece of literature. The fact that it calls for concentration should not, even in 1939, condemn it.

But his style is flexible. Since leaving office he has been writing articles of great directness and punch, saying succinctly and in graphic homely phrases what millions of his fellow countrymen wish they had the power to express. That faculty is said to be a kind of poetry and it has a wider, if more ephemeral, circulation than the metrical variety. If Duff Cooper could be separated from his record and from his rebellion against the dominant figure of Neville Chamberlain, a poll on the propositions he has set out in his journalism would yield, I believe, an overwhelming affirmative vote. Let us hope that an incidental advantage has been to compensate him for the loss of Admiralty House and a first lord's salary.

Years ago the House of Commons was discussing the proposed demolition of Waterloo Bridge. As might be expected, Duff Cooper took the aesthetic line. Why, he asked, destroy this historic monument when it may well be that to the Englishman abroad his chief memory of "home" is the river front containing Waterloo Bridge, Somerset House, the Embankment, and Westminster? His intellectual interests embrace the theater. Often he can be seen sitting solemnly beside his wife in a box in some fashionable theater. She, too, watches the stage with an expert eye, for before the First German War she played with distinction the part of the lovely nun in Max Reinhardt's *Miracle*.

He did not take a long rest after Munich. When the House was discussing the financial advance to Czechoslovakia he said it was a sad day for the House of Commons and the sooner it was over the better. His most famous postresignation attack occurred during the debate on the 1939 naval estimates on the morrow of the ides of March. He answered Winston Churchill's objection to the proposal to scrap battleships three years from that date: "Something will happen. A great deal must happen before the year 1942. *Either a fearful disaster will have befallen the world,* or we shall have moved into a happier period. Either the all for which we have striven for so long will have been lost and peace will have disappeared from the world, or else peace will be better assured than it is today. One thing is absolutely certain. This period of tension and anxiety cannot continue."

He proceeded to criticize the Anglo-German Naval Treaty. When we had a curvilinear coast line to defend and needed also to be ready to send a fleet to South Africa, the Indian Ocean, the Far East, and the West Indies, the agreed ratio of 100 to 35 ceased to be impressive. A fellow Conservative interrupted to ask what terms more favorable to ourselves Germany would have been likely to accept. Duff Cooper retorted that our allowing

Germany to have a navy at all was an act of generosity of which she had gradually taken advantage. He went on: "Whether it is a great advantage to have a treaty with Germany of any kind I am extremely doubtful, and I have always been. Indeed, I consider any agreement that Hitler signs is not worth the paper it is written on, while *that thrice-perjured traitor and breaker of oaths is at the head of the German state."*

As the Munich agreement had the day before been torn to shreds, nobody protested—either in England or in Germany. On April 28, 1939, Hitler took another step toward war and denounced the Anglo-German Naval Treaty. Once again Duff Cooper was fully vindicated in a period shorter than he himself could have foreseen.

The war which he had treated as virtually inevitable began for Britain on September 3rd. Perhaps one would have expected Duff Cooper to be among the first choices in a war government. He had risked everything because, a year before, he had declined to trust the word of a proved traitor. Churchill and Eden were marched inevitably into the administration. But Chamberlain managed for the time to pass over a critic less conspicuous but just as sincere as Winston Churchill.

Duff Cooper might legitimately feel aggrieved. But he has shown no bitterness. On the contrary, he has acclaimed by tongue and pen the admirable firmness of Neville Chamberlain since hostilities began. He is at the moment a watchdog of his country's resolution.

The war had hardly been in progress for a month when Lloyd George caused him to extemporize a counterattack. The elderly but vigorous ex-premier risked being charged with pique at his own exclusion from the government. He said in the House that it was clear that detailed terms for peace were going to come from some source and he urged that the government should not be in a hurry to reject them. He asked that Parliament should be given an opportunity to discuss any "detailed declarations" that might be forthcoming and also that there should be a secret session of the House of Commons.

Duff Cooper rose at once, but so did Mr. Chamberlain. Being prime minister, the latter "caught the Speaker's eye." In a short, mild statement he refused a secret session but assured Lloyd George that the government would not be in any hurry to answer a peace proposal; the possibility of any proposals coming was purely hypothetical; so he could not say at any length what might be done.

By the time the prime minister had finished Duff Cooper's temperature had gone soaring. After regretting that a secret session had been rejected, he said that Lloyd George's speech was the strongest possible argument in favor of one. His words, said Duff Cooper, would be reported and misrepresented. They would go out to the world as a suggestion of surrender. Would the German government offer terms which did anything less than register the astounding victory they had just won over Poland and stamp that victory on the face of Europe? And even supposing terms were offered more favorable than anyone imagined, they would be embodied in a treaty containing the same signature as signed the Munich agreement. The prime minister had said that that signature was not worth the paper it was written on. No peace was possible with the present German government.

This was a fiery performance. He may have strained the meaning of Lloyd George's language. But he well knew the use that might be made of anything that sounded like weakening from the lips of one with such immense authority as Lloyd George. To such lengths of consistency—such salutary lengths—does Duff Cooper's hatred of the Nazi tyranny carry him. With such ease can he improvise a retort to the most formidable of opponents.

It is worth while observing that Duff Cooper is one of the few speakers to whom Winston Churchill makes a point of listening. The reason must be twofold—sense and style. Nobody could deny him the first quality in the harsh light of recent events. As to the second, Duff Cooper can actually do one thing that is denied to Churchill: he can rehearse a theme of complex gravity without the anchor of a manuscript. He is a throwback to the more combative age of controversy in which Churchill is rooted. His posture and gestures are martial. As he speaks he tosses back his head like a high-mettled charger. That is the kind of personality to appeal to a descendant of Marlborough.

After the war whose shadows we have, as Duff Cooper so fatefully predicted, just entered, the old forms of government may or may not survive in Britain. If during this calamity they do live on in some form, however unlike their prewar shape, Duff Cooper should undoubtedly be summoned to administer some department. He has vigor and a clear-sighted patriotism. I hope I have shown that he could summarize in lucid and inspiring language the cause which has driven us to arms.

Where Duff Cooper may fail in a democratic community is in the limited personal appeal he can make. He is not a man to mingle with the mob. He could not endure to drink with vulgarians or to swap silly stories with fools. But these defects carry qualities which fully counterbalance them. He has a spirit above the lower manifestations of ambition. His first ambition is to deal honorably with his own conscience and to obey the guidance of his own intelligence. If the fulfillment of one's main ambition is a ground for satisfaction, Duff Cooper should be a happy man.

CHAPTER IX

SIR KINGSLEY WOOD
The Man on the Flying Trapeze

BY THE end of the Kaiser's War in November, 1918, Great Britain had a great and powerful air force consisting of tens of thousands of machines. In 1914 flying was militarily little more than an experimental adjunct to the navy and the army. Under the pressure of a little more than four years' hostilities it had become a force of awful achievement and pregnant possibilities.

Britain had become supreme in the air. This supremacy was forced upon her in self-defense. Early in the war Zeppelins were able to fly by night over England and hover silently in the darkness above the targets they had chosen. Then destruction would suddenly descend upon a city half asleep and more than half unsuspecting. England came to know the meaning of the terror that flieth by night.

But the power of defense rose to meet this horror. The Zeppelin was mastered by fighter aircraft. Marauding airships were no longer sent by the German command to their certain end. The most vivid spectacle I have ever seen was a Zeppelin at night falling to the earth in flames —an experience I had at the age of sixteen when I was still a schoolboy.

A raid was in progress but our airplanes had learned their own power. From the ground we saw the progress of the attack on the dark and detestable airship. The airplane flew beside the monster pouring bullets into the envelope. A flame suddenly appeared at one end of the Zeppelin; then sped along its entire length.

In a few seconds the enemy burst into fire which momentarily illuminated the countryside as though the sun had by a miracle risen at midnight. The fiery mass crumpled into a colossal swollen L and the whole lurid ruin fell slowly to the earth half a dozen miles away.

The cheers of victory—somebody else's victory—rang through the dormitories of the school. We thought little or nothing about the frightful end of the Zeppelin's crew. For the rest of one night we could sleep in absolute security.

But the German ingenuity was not exhausted. The Zeppelin as a night raider was defeated only to be succeeded by the bombing airplane which carried out its most effective attacks by day. I witnessed from afar a little of the progress of twenty German aircraft to their objective —the metropolis. On that particular occasion London suffered seriously. Only one of the twenty was brought down.

That was the summer of 1918. But before long the advance of the French, Americans, and British against their armies became too serious a preoccupation for the Germans to continue spending their energies on their not very successful or gallant attempt at terrorizing the civilian population of Great Britain. All available German aircraft were needed on the western front for an equally unsuccessful effort to stem the flowing tide.

For the greater part of the war most of Belgium was in the hands of the enemy. He was also established far in French territory. So, in those days when the range of the airplane was vastly shorter than today, he could raid British and French centers of population with far greater facility.

We did not retaliate on German civilians. Yet the Armistice of November 11th saved them from the most terrible retribution. At the very moment of the "cease fire" hundreds of British Handley-Page bombers were drawn up on French soil ready to bring to the people of Germany terrors of a dimension unknown to Paris or London. As I write these words they are still without a taste of them. And we hope it may not become necessary for the British Royal Air Force to inflict it.

At this moment—just before midnight—the radio announcer has told us that the dance band will play "something prewar"—"The Lights of London." The absolute black-out over the whole of Britain and Northern Ireland is one of the elements in our recovery of that aerial supremacy which we lost after 1918. It is a mildly depressing feature of the present hostilities—endurable, but exasperating. The normally brilliant glare of London streets excites and delights us. But now Piccadilly after the setting of the sun is nothing more than a gloomy canyon. Imagine Broadway and Fifth Avenue dark as the grave from sunset to sunrise!

Till 1933 when the Nazis reached the seats of power in Germany and Hitler with his lieutenant Goering thereupon began building his huge air fleet, the Royal Air Force remained a faint shadow of its earlier terrific size. What there was of it was efficient and zealous for experiment. Annual air pageants were held, at which weird and wonderful new types would cruise over the heads of wonder-struck spectators.

The air force patrolled the outlying districts of the

empire and succeeded thus in saving the Imperial Exchequer many millions of pounds and the army many hundreds of lives. Its activities were accurately described as "police action." Seldom did the flying machines from the West need actually to bomb the evacuated homesteads of violent and disorderly tribesmen in Iraq or upon the northwest frontier of India. Their presence alone was usually enough to restore order. These functions were for years the main activity of the air force.

At the opening of the Disarmament Conference in February, 1932, the British government sought without success to achieve an air convention. None of the powers could agree. The French, who were the most prominent exponents of the brilliant idea of an International Air Police Force, could not persuade enough of the other states to solve in this way the problems of disarmament, security, and unbridled national sovereignty.

Yet the problem haunted the mind of the British government. Baldwin, in a celebrated speech on November 10, 1932, told the House of Commons that, in his opinion, European civilization would be "wiped out" by the next war and "by no force more than by the air force." In the same speech he said, "Whatever the man in the street may be told to the contrary the bomber is bound to get through."

There seem, after all, to be a number of answers. Baldwin, as he himself later seemed to acknowledge, should have said "*a* bomber" and not "*the* bomber." If you can make sure of destroying fifty bombers out of every hundred that attack you the enemy will not be able to sustain his attack. His moral and material losses will be too high. And if the enemy knows that you can give him as much, if not more, than you will get from him, his generosity may not be too forthcoming.

Goering and Hitler rearmed in secret and finally exchanged secrecy for boasting. They spent on arms the equivalent of five billion dollars a year! Much of this treasure was devoted to the Nazi Air Force, which grew and grew like the stomach of Hitler's fiıst lieutenant. It far outstripped in size the force of any other single European power.

At length Baldwin was persuaded to give a pledge that Britain should have an air force which would have "parity with any air force within striking distance of our shores." Later a controversy developed whether parity should be measured in numbers. It has long been claimed that, plane for plane and pilot for pilot, the Royal Air Force is greatly superior to the German. But such qualitative superiority would be a small consolation if the ratio of numbers between Germany and Britain was three, five, or even ten to one.

The pace of the arms race quickened and grew hotter. Plans of expansion on an unbelievable scale were conceived by the British government. Capital expenditure to be spread over several years was authorized to the extent of ten billion dollars. But while the finance and the resources were there, the things lacking were the factories.

They began to come, at first slowly. After the crisis over Czechoslovakia in September, 1938, the plans for rearmament were further enlarged. By the beginning of 1939 the democracy of Britain began seriously to overhaul the dictatorship of Germany. The lathes were turning at full speed, the factories swung into full production. New factories leapt out of the ground.

France, too, recovered her capacity for arms production.

The combined aerial might if the western democracies could at last, not only qualitatively but quantitatively as well, look Goering's air force in the face.

Numbers cannot be given. But, when the whole history of the past few months can be written, the historian will be able to make the student gasp at the speed and dimensions of the sudden British effort in the air. Not least vital has been the excellence of the training given to the personnel. That training has always been of the highest order. Before a man can qualify in England as a pilot he must fly a great total of hours.

In the most important commodity—petrol—Britain has taken care to supply herself generously. The home production of oil from coal is infinitesimal. But behind the shield of the British Navy, in war no less than in peace, tanker after tanker conveys to our ports an abundance of the commodity which feeds the Royal Air Force with its motive power. The private citizen's first experience of rationing is in respect to petrol. He is now allowed about a fifth of his normal consumption. But the three fighting services are amply supplied.

Marshal Goering has graciously promised that the "war which England has desired shall shower upon her from the skies." We still await an installment of the Blitzkrieg. We are still waiting for a sample of the terrible experience of Poland. Daily the weather becomes more wintry and less favorable to aerial attack on this country. But the vigilance of the watchers and defenders is never abated for an instant. Hourly the production of new British aircraft and the training of fresh British pilots increases in intensity. Most encouraging of all to the Allied cause, the American Neutrality Act has been so modified—to the surprise of many English people—that we can count on a bottomless arsenal of ammunition and, above all, aircraft on the other side of the Atlantic.

Canada, too, is a safe center for the advanced training of airmen from the self-governing dominions of the British Commonwealth. Canada, Australia, and New Zealand provide a tough type of manhood, less urbanized than the youth of the United Kingdom. But let no one forget that life in Britain is still largely a thing of the open air. Agriculture is still our greatest industry and employs 1,300,000 men.

At the present moment the material forces of the two sides in the Second German War may be sufficiently well balanced to discourage Hitler from any enterprise which would provoke instant retaliation. But the probability is that the raids will come, and on a great scale. The fighter command in England is spoiling to show what it can do against a really serious attack.

Meanwhile I beg my readers to understand that we should prefer to win this war without seeing London, Cambridge, Oxford, and the centers in the Midlands and the North reduced to powder. The war is not "phony" merely because it fails to provide neutrals with a series of catastrophic and spectacular incidents. Ask the navy and the mercantile marine whether the war is real. Ask a sailor whose ship has been dispatched by a U-boat. Ask a pilot who has bombed a German submarine.

The pacific character of the leaflet raids which the Royal Air Force has carried out over Germany on such a great scale has yielded a crop of stories. From one such raid two pilots returned, one far earlier, the other much later than was expected. "Why are you so early?" snapped out the commanding officer to the first. "I forgot to use my dispersing apparatus, sir. When I got over X, I let the

leaflets fall in parcels." "Very careless of you," said the
C.O.; "why, you might have hurt somebody!"

The other he reprimanded, "You're disgracefully late.
Why are you so behind the others in returning?" "I'm
sorry, sir," said the pilot. "To make sure they should be
delivered I popped each of them through a letter box!"

These agreeable legends underrate the courage needed
to fly on this persuasive mission hundreds of miles into
enemy territory with or without the accompaniment of
antiaircraft fire.

Time must bring the western democracies an air
strength of overwhelming power. *That is the object of
our policy and production.* Whether the power will have
to be used against the heart of Germany, and, if so, how,
are the secrets of the Higher Command, of the War Cabinet in general, and of the secretary of state for air in
particular.

This minister is the Right Honorable Sir Kingsley
Wood, who, in spite of a diminutive stature and various
comic physical characteristics, is a serious candidate for the
premiership. After fifty-eight years of life he is plump, rotund, and chubby. He was as pacific as any other member
of the government. When before the war a particularly
pugnacious politician was urging a "firm stand" against
Germany and was saying that war was inevitable and anyway better than continued humiliation and repeated surrender, Sir Kingsley Wood quietly replied, "Maybe; but
there will be pain and tears."

That is his serious side, which is less frequently in evidence. "This is somebody," you will say as you watch him
beaming behind his spectacles, "who is ready for a good
joke. Indeed, I am sure he will oblige at the slightest
provocation." And when in a moment his high-pitched

chuckle is audible you are pleased to see how right you were. Only the mustache and glasses distinguish him from an animated version of one of the stone cherubs so popular among Georgian architects.

But Sir Kingsley cannot be thus lightly dismissed. He is one of the ablest of administrators, with a personality so agreeable that he seems to create his own good luck as he marches on. To many he is entertaining; to none is he offensive. Separated from his mental capacities his physique is a subject for comedy. But he has won for himself great renown as a ministerial go-getter and to him success is as spontaneous as the floating of a football on a pond.

Sir Kingsley Wood has been fortunate in that he has never had to endure the ordeals that other aspirants to high office have suffered. He and good fortune are on the best of terms. He is a most unusual type for prominence in the Tory party—or, indeed, for any modern English political notoriety. He is the son of a Wesleyan clergyman, was a former practicing solicitor, and is without the background of famous school or ancient university.

But he early showed that success was likely to become a habit with him, as he greatly distinguished himself in his law examinations. He served a political apprenticeship on the London County Council from 1911 to 1918. During those years he busied himself with committees on building, old-age pensions, insurance, and separation allowances. These activities might seem humdrum, but at the end of the war he was in the forefront of a movement to persuade Lloyd George to establish a Ministry of Health.

His work had had a direction and unity of purpose. The Ministry of Health came into being to supersede the old Local Government Board. In the 1918 election Kingsley Wood was elected as Conservative member of Parliament for a working-class division. On this seat he has remained enthroned ever since. Once—in 1929—he was nearly shaken off his perch. But he is now one of the very few men whose personality and reputation make it possible to set aside private electoral worries.

But the earlier need to fight hard in his own constituency has kept him nearer the public heart than the remote contacts with a few important constituents that are all that is necessary in a "safe seat." Lloyd George, likewise a solicitor and a dissenter, has always set a high value on Kingsley Wood's capacity. His knighthood was awarded during Lloyd George's administration.

All through the past twenty years Kingsley Wood has reflected the beams of Fortune's smile. He has made good friends of event and circumstance, and his career in office illustrates a luck as conspicuous as the ambition of other men.

Directly he entered the House he had the opportunity of learning the work of the ministry which he had helped to create and over which he would one day preside. He served as parliamentary private secretary to both Dr. Addison and the late Sir Alfred Mond (later Lord Melchett, the head of the huge Imperial Chemical Industries), who were successively minister of health.

Being an opponent of the dispatch of the Coalition, Kingsley Wood could not be given office by Bonar Law. But in 1924 he was made parliamentary secretary to the Ministry of Health. Here he was efficient and unruffled by opposition. He enjoyed, moreover, the good fortune of having as his chief Neville Chamberlain. If he had any merits, four years and a half of co-operation in the same ministry would reveal them to the future Man of Munich.

Later he and his party joined effectively in the hunt of the Labor government.

By speech and by question he showed himself to be an expert tormentor. His touch was light and impudent—as comic as a tickle, but far more damaging. When an official veil was being drawn during question time over a matter that was notoriously causing friction within the government, Kingsley Wood leaned across from the Opposition Front Bench and innocently asked the prime minister with mock solicitude, "No trouble over this, I hope?"

But with the formation of the emergency National government the amnesty to Ramsay MacDonald's most hostile opponents had to be complete. Kingsley Wood was made parliamentary secretary to the Board of Education till the general election which came two months later.

In an administration of unqualified Conservatism he would doubtless have had high office at once. But there were "National Labor" and "Liberal National" ambitions which Ramsay MacDonald, Baldwin, and Simon had to satisfy as well. So after the election Sir Kingsley had to be satisfied with the comparatively minor office of the Post Office. This position, however, was one of growing importance.

Despite financial crises and industrial depression, the work of the Post Office in Britain expanded uniformly. The postmaster general was also in a certain degree the minister ultimately responsible for the British Broadcasting Corporation, whose range and influence were now entering their stage of maximum development. The minute Sir Kingsley Wood had to work in double harness with the gigantic autocrat, the director general of the BBC, Sir John Reith.

Double bass and high falsetto contrived a passable harmony; some credit must go to the postmaster general for his patient relationships with one who had the embarrassing reputation of being a superman. Broadcasting in Britain has been admired because of its noncommercial character. Over here you cannot "buy" or "sell" time. When much later the moment came for a regular service of television the BBC quickly generated this child. So sound was its parentage that the supremacy of British television was universally accepted. Television was rapidly becoming a commercial proposition. Substations for the radiation of sight programs were being arranged in the provincial centers. The programs were often magnificent and more attractive than many a good film.

Hitler's war temporarily stopped this most exciting and wonderful development. Hard luck, John Bull! In this field you undoubtedly led the world. Neither Reith nor Kingsley Wood has retained his old office. But to them must go the main credit for the fruitful flowering of British broadcasting.

While Kingsley Wood was in office the purveying of postage stamps and the acceptance of telegrams ceased being the duty of rude and inferior civil servants and became a polite amenity. So acceptably did he dispense the services offered by the Post Office and the BBC and so rapidly did these two services expand in importance that he was, though still only postmaster general, brought into the Cabinet in December, 1933. He became the managing director of an installment of agreeable Socialism.

Years before—in 1928—his ability had been recognized by a privy councilorship; and now his fortune brought him into the executive. His ready tongue disarmed

EVENING TOURS
SIEGFRIED
LINE
AND BEYOND

CHARING ✠ 3073

British Combine Photo

Kingsley Wood (center), Secretary of State for Air, plump, rotund and
bby, has the grave responsibility of directing the activities of England's
al armada. A serious aspirant for the premiership, a shrewd politician,
"he has the invaluable asset of a perpetually youthful spirit."

would-be critics and enhanced his parliamentary reputation.

Round about this time the government took the responsibility of examining correspondence from England to the Irish Free State containing bets for the Irish Sweepstake. An opponent of the betting regulations asked furiously, "Does the Post Office need any extra staff to tamper with the correspondence of private individuals?" Kingsley Wood replied without a moment's hesitation, "No, sir. We take it in our stride!"

When Baldwin became prime minister he elevated Kingsley Wood to the Ministry of Health. His luck should again be observed. A great drive for slum clearance had been begun, but the legislation which inaugurated it caused much bitterness among property owners. If an official of the Ministry of Health found premises "unfit for human habitation," they were to be demolished without compensation to the landlord other than "site value." So a mass of rickety, lousy, evil-smelling structures were pulled down and the bricks that had harbored the lice were often ground to powder. But consider the anguish of men and women with all their savings invested in house property whose habitability was thus determined by a bureaucrat!

This policy caused the greatest resentment among many Conservatives who, as champions of the rights of private ownership, complained that property was being confiscated without adequate compensation. But this storm buffeted Sir Hilton Young, Kingsley Wood's predecessor, and had died down by the time Wood succeeded to the post. He arrived at the lucky moment and war saved him from being the scapegoat of infuriated property owners.

Again Fortune laughed with her puckish favorite. Dissatisfaction and misgiving grew about the conduct of the program for air expansion. It was alleged that, in spite of mountainous estimates for air rearmament, we were lagging further and further behind Germany. Lord Swinton (formerly Sir Philip Lloyd-Greame and then Sir Philip Cunliffe-Lister), however efficient he may have been as the flywheel of a department, lacked the manners of the natural democrat. He was abrupt and inaccessible.

Men disliked being made to feel inferior or to hear their inquiries brushed aside with apparent contempt. Lord Swinton was unable to help giving the most unfortunate impression. Moreover, though the head of a great spending department, he had chosen to accept a viscounty.

The House of Commons controls finance and it is always right that the political heads of departments that swallow much of the revenue should sit in that House. There they will have to face the people's elected representatives. Mr. Chamberlain defended his noble minister for a time and then found it would be wisest to let him go. For a successor, a man who would be certain to make the heavens hum, he chose Sir Kingsley Wood in May, 1938.

Less than a year and a half has passed, but, whereas twelve months ago we were wringing our hands over our alleged weakness in the air, today our bombers must be a source of anxiety to Hitler. Hundreds of them are at this moment lying ready on French soil beneath a cunning camouflage of leafy branches. We are reputed to have an aerial armada of Spitfires. These fighter machines are easily maneuverable and yet streak through the sky at unbelievable speeds. The latest types are even more formidable. Each squadron in the Royal Air Force has behind it a perpetually increasing depth of reserve machines.

Our power for strict self-defense is known to be considerable and has already given several unpleasant surprises to the enemy's sky marauders. Our capacity for doing injury to others is now beyond being measured. That capacity, for reasons I have given, is bound to grow and grow.

Of course, this change has not been wrought exclusively by the magic of Kingsley Wood. No doubt, his most constant satellites would like us to think so, but any such illusion must be rejected. Much of the planning for expansion was accomplished before Kingsley Wood became secretary of state for air. The designs of the great new factories were approved before the responsibility for their products became his. Since he has had the power, those factories have been completed and have come into full production.

He is reaping a rich harvest, all of which he did not sow himself. Unavoidably credit is attaching to the lucky little minister for the preparations set in hand by his predecessors. It may be said that only results matter and not the winning or losing of laurels.

But no one should deprive Kingsley Wood of the credit for furthering the acceleration. Under his supervision and the dynamic impulse which Lloyd George long ago saw he possessed, the air expansion has proceeded with unpredicted smoothness and rapidity.

Men like working for Sir Kingsley and he can stimulate them to their best efforts. With subordinates and deputations he is brisk without being brusque. He does not waste time and, though he is often the victim of fatigue, he listens keenly to what is said and impresses those who wait upon him that their submissions are not futile.

He is an example of the triumph of inner force over

externals. An effort has to be made by any stranger before he is able to take seriously this friendly but imperative sprite who shrills out his jests and commands in the popular tones of the London suburbs.

But while he saw the skies darkening with the armadas of which he was the political master he kept one ear studiously to the ground. Not only is he a born administrator—a departmental winner—but he is the keenest and most cunning of politicians. Since February, 1938, he has been grand master of the Primrose League. This was a political body formed many years ago to perpetuate the memory of Disraeli, the greatest of Conservative prime ministers. So the fortunes of the Conservative party are very dear to Kingsley Wood.

It has never been denied that after Munich Sir Kingsley began to urge the prime minister to seize upon the moment of his maximum popularity. Part of the country was hailing him as the architect of abiding peace. He should, whispered Kingsley Wood, hold a general election and so cash in on peace.

Kingsley Wood is said to have taken this plea beyond the confidential confines of the Cabinet and to have trotted round the lobbies of the House of Commons on his opportunist errand. Some thought it was an excellent idea. Others felt their stomachs turning with disgust.

On the second day of the Munich debate a dramatic speech was made by the Conservative Sir Sidney Herbert. He rarely spoke, and this speech turned out to be his last. Few men could have said what he said so effectively. He was a devoted servant of the Conservative party, a man of birth, breeding, wealth, and education. He had lost a leg through an operation and was correctly considered by many to be a dying man. He spoke in a passion of rage.

After calling Munich "a grave and desperate humiliation" he said, "There are also rumors that if things go smoothly and favorably and comfortably, there will be a general election. Now I do not care at this time about my own party, or any other party, but there could be no greater iniquity in the world than to force a general election on the people of this country at this moment. . . . The government have a fine majority. . . .

"At the expense of much dishonor," he went on, "we have gained a temporary respite of peace. In the name of all that is decent let us use that for rearmament. But if we have a general election with all the stupid bitterness which occurs at every general election . . . who will gain anything by it? I am sure the prime minister, whose integrity and character I know and admire, would never give his countenance to such a solution. *There may be some tiny Tammany Hall ring who want it* but my solution would be quite different. . . . I ask the prime minister to make his government really national, to broaden its basis, to invite the Labor party into it, to invite above all the trade-union leaders into it. . . ."

Thus was a mortal blow struck at Kingsley Wood's interesting electoral plans. Thanks to this dying declaration and to other speeches, he was compelled to see his design of capitalizing public ignorance and uninformed gratitude fading out of the realm of possibility.

Everybody concluded that the main link in the "tiny Tammany Hall ring" was Kingsley Wood. The prime minister did not take the advice offered by the dying patriot to form a broad-based government. But neither did he heed Kingsley Wood's politic urgencies to go while the going seemed good. Sir Kingsley seems to have been, for once in his life, too clever by half, to have erred on the side of astuteness.

This episode was a sorry sideslip, but only a momentary misfortune. What he had conceived as a skillful and popular move turned out not to be so very popular after all. But Kingsley Wood is not given to brooding on failure or miscalculation. The chances are that he has already forgotten how some dull souls failed to agree that the snatching of a party advantage was the thing that mattered so tremendously. Perhaps he will even chuckle at their ineptitude. Were not their objections blind, quixotic, and suicidal? He could be seen scanning the horizon for the next main chance. "Never mind, prime minister, we shall come again," he might easily have said, for this amiable nonconformist suggests the language of the race course. He is a political stayer. When peace returns Kingsley Wood should be there serving his party as well as he has been serving his country.

But above all he excels as an executive administrator. Kingsley Wood, if faced with any choice, quickly makes his decision and explains good-naturedly the reasons which have brought him to make it. Then he cheerfully looks around him for the next problem to solve.

We can make use of such men even when they are greatly enamored of politics for its own sake. When the Conservatives have again to choose a new leader Sir Kingsley Wood's claims will have to be treated seriously. He has the invaluable asset of a perpetually youthful spirit.

CHAPTER X

SIR SAMUEL HOARE
John Bull in Office

IN THE War Cabinet one of the ministers with no specified duties is the "lord privy seal," Sir Samuel Hoare. As long ago as 1884 the duties formerly assigned to this post were abolished by act of Parliament. But the holder of this curiosity among ancient offices has often been entrusted with important work requiring the attention of a minister of the crown. The main characteristics of the present holder of the office are preciseness, integrity, and ambition.

Sir Samuel Hoare is a remarkable contrast to the minister just described—Sir Kingsley Wood. Set these two right honorable gentlemen to run a hundred-yard race and you need have no doubt of the result. Though Sir Kingsley is a little junior in age and considerably younger in mind he could hardly be a match for his spare lean opponent. Sir Samuel, though nearly sixty, still skates with the slim economy of movement which enabled him to represent Oxford University. He can hardly have acquired an extra pound's weight in the past forty years.

He has, moreover, a distinguished record as a performer at racquets and lawn tennis; his prominence at Wimbledon ceremonies is a tribute to his personal prowess. In the days of peace he would often be seen there presiding over the award of trophies to the American champions who have so many times swept the board.

Sir Kingsley Wood and Sir Samuel Hoare are serious competitors in the race for that Conservative leadership which Sir Samuel so openly desires. It is possible that neither will come in first. But if they were left alone in the field Sir Kingsley might turn the event into a procession of which he did not form the rear guard.

Hoare is an enormously successful person. But, unlike Kingsley Wood, he is not a spontaneous generator of his own success. He has to be buoyed up and propelled forward by cork, oars, sails, and steam. He gives an impression of intense cerebral labor. That impression cannot be altogether correct as he was a "double first" at Oxford, which certainly implies mental agility. If he is not by nature a quick thinker, he must have trained his mind to move at a fair speed.

He is serious and desperately sensitive. He is the soul of care and caution. His audience listen to his governess-like voice as he reads an answer to a parliamentary question or slowly unfolds the argument of an important speech, and while listening feel the strain of his caution. It is another symptom of his ambition. He is taking such immense trouble in order to disarm damaging criticism. He is laboriously laying down the road for his own progress.

Before we dissect further let us notice his features. Wide-open eyes peer at the future in questioning bewilderment. His eyebrows suggest a huge interrogation mark. He often speaks at the greatest length, so he has constantly to clear his throat. It is a peculiar and alarming sound—for all the world as though a spinster were flying into a passion of rage. Many members of the House of Commons lolling slumbrously on all sides have been startled out of their postprandial dreams by this clap of thunder interrupting his slow and measured progress.

Has Sir Samuel the right to take himself and his career so seriously? He has taken but one toss in his ride along the highroad of fame; but, as we shall see directly, that was such a painful and heavy fall that it may have dislocated his prospects for good. The marvel is that he climbed back into the saddle so soon and with so few manifestly broken bones. His record is enough to show that he is one of those who are born naturally to assume a respectable responsibility.

Hoare was born in 1880. He migrated from Harrow to New College, Oxford, about the turn of the century. There he distinguished himself athletically and academically. Probably his contemporaries wearied of wondering if Samuel Hoare could ever do wrong or make a mistake. Perhaps at some early moment he consciously formulated an ambition to have a hand in the changes which nature and history would decree, for he had inherited from a forebear, Elizabeth Fry, an instinct and a feeling for reform. She was one of the most famous of English prison reformers. Before her day the cruelties of our prison life were a disgrace to a civilized community.

In 1909 Hoare married Lady Maud Lygon, sister of Lord Beauchamp. In 1906 he had fought and lost Ipswich as a Conservative. But Lady Maud had not long to wait before she became the wife of a member.

In 1910 this exemplary young statesman began his unbroken representation of the cast-iron Tory London borough of Chelsea. And for nearly thirty years he has had no electoral worries.

Chelsea is a medley of artists and of aristocrats, of comfortable affluence and hidden poverty, of eighteenth century architecture and twentieth century experiments in concrete. It can give its Conservative member little anxiety; it needs no special attention.

Half the population of Chelsea is in flux, the other half is rooted to the Embankment, which fringes the Thames, and the neighborhood of the King's Road, which runs from Putney to Buckingham Palace. A few of the inhabitants may talk revolution but a vast majority will infallibly vote Tory. So Sir Samuel has been able to apply himself to his own advancement.

Baldwin, his fellow Harrovian, saw in him much that he could respect—learning, high connections, a mind free from emotional tides or stubborn prejudice. Whether he felt the same enthusiasm for Hoare's naïve disclosure of his own ambition or his ultimate lack of the steel of resolution may be a matter for doubt.

During the war he acquired a mass of foreign decorations. By its end, aged thirty-eight, he was a lieutenant colonel. He could go back to the House of Commons and combine with Lord Winterton and the future Lord Halifax in a team of knowing "old parliamentary hands." Lord Winterton, being an Irish peer, was entitled to sit in the House of Commons. He embodies the traditional notion of the fox-hunting aristocrat. The assiduous and conscientious dullness of Hoare and Halifax was relieved by the breezy arrogance of Winterton.

In 1922 Bonar Law, prime minister for a few months, jumped the young man of forty-two right into the Air Ministry. Though this was an astonishing event even at that moment of miraculous promotions, it was not so surprising in the departmental circumstances of 1922. The Air Ministry was threatened with dissolution or merger with the War Office. It had ceased for the time being to occupy a position of vital importance. The Royal Air Force was a mere skeleton of the vast machine which in the war had won tactical pre-eminence by 1918.

But Hoare soaked himself in the work of his department and, when its extinction seemed near, he procured the survival of its separate identity by plaintive and lachrymose entreaties. Baldwin put him into his Cabinet when he succeeded Bonar Law. Again from 1924 to 1929 Sam Hoare held this same office. The reinstatement of the senior brains of the Tory party did not seem to dislodge him from the niche he had won for himself in their counsels.

By 1931 he had become significant enough to be one of the few heads of the Conservative party who arranged the coalition with Ramsay MacDonald, Herbert Samuel, and John Simon. They made him secretary of state for India after the general election. For three and a half years he sustained the weight of this high office while the greatest of all constitutional bills, the Government of India Act, was passed into law.

Hoare was to the fore the whole time, the utterly reliable instrument of Baldwin's determination to seem generous to India. First there was the constitution of the Joint Select Committee, then its taking of evidence, when Hoare had to answer hundreds of questions. Then came an unexpected episode when he was charged by Churchill with trying to prejudice the witnesses who were to be called before the committee.

There was next the framing of the bill itself with its four hundred clauses. The bill was drawn, of course, by government draftsmen, but the minister had to master the legislation before he could pilot it through the House. Finally, there was the protracted series of debates upon the bill itself, a long second reading, the interminable committee stage taken, not in a "standing committee," but on the floor of the House, when every clause was liable to be criticized or recast and any number of new clauses might be added.

That did not end the labor. There remained the further possibilities of revision on the report stage, and last of all the third reading. In this elaborate way does the Commons safeguard itself against hasty legislation. But yet another safeguard exists in the House of Lords, whither legislation passed in the Lower House has finally to go for more debates and more revision!

Hoare's health did not last the full course. He was slightly run down as the committee stage advanced and his work was done by the undersecretary of state. But till then he had gone ahead with the business of standing up to Churchill and the diehards of whom Winston became the intellectual chief. The tough business of building a constitution for a subcontinent was rudely interrupted by Churchill's charge of breach of privilege. The Committee of Privileges cleared Sam Hoare completely.

In a debate on their report Amery was speaking. He said of Churchill that he was so jealous of right and justice that he might have entered the controversy saying *"Fiat justitia; ruat caelum."* Churchill rashly ejaculated, "Translate!" Amery said, "I will translate it, and in order that my right honorable friend can understand it I will translate it in the vernacular—'If I can trip up Sam the government's bust!'"

The huge laugh that followed showed that Amery was expressing a widely held opinion. Hoare and Churchill are not mutually sympathetic men. This old antipathy has now been submerged in the face of a common enemy

of their country. Churchill and Hoare today work together in the same War Cabinet. But during the Indian
controversy Hoare can hardly have enjoyed Churchill's
persistent criticisms.

In the end, however, these hostile moves really helped
Hoare. In the minds of the overwhelming majority he
advanced from a position of negative innocence to positive virtue.

No one who listened to his expositions of the India bill
could doubt that he was dealing with a matter of infinite
complexity demanding indefatigable industry. As his thin
voice set out line upon line, precept upon precept, here a
little and there a little, those who heard the gradual progress may have fancied that they were listening to a strain-
ing steel hawser creaking and groaning as it dragged the
massive argument uphill.

There was rooted and sometimes well-informed objection to much that he said, but Hoare was able to wear
down the antagonisms of some of his audience by the
simple and time-honored expedient of boring them. Nobody claimed for him that his performance was in any
way stimulating. But his admirers—and he was not without them—could say to one another, "Read Sam Hoare
tomorrow in Hansard [the official report of parliamentary
proceedings] and you will see that not a word is out of
place." Faint praise perhaps, but not so faint as to damn
him completely.

The late Lord Curzon said of Hoare that he seemed to
be descended from a long line of maiden aunts. Certainly
his expressions of sour disapproval lend some color to the
comparison. As he has severely plied his horn-rimmed
spectacles the irreverent have muttered, "What's trou-
bling Prunes and Prisms Hoare?"

But the success of this period of his career often made the world he surveyed seem a sunny place. In 1935 Baldwin replaced Simon at the Foreign Office by Hoare. Many critics who had found the Simon regime less and less tolerable were pleased that the foreign secretaryship was to go to a man who seemed to have a decisive mind and positive initiative. He was going to give them the shock of their lives. For there now follows the most astonishing story—a true story—of "sudden and unpredictable collapse."

Some kind of crisis was bound to come. Italy was openly plotting to invade Ethiopia and Eden was striving to dissuade the Italians. If persuasion failed, the members of the League of Nations could do one of three things: they could condemn and, having uttered their condemnation, they could repeat the practical inertia they had exhibited about Manchuria; they could attempt action which might succeed if given enough time; or they could risk the wrath of Mussolini and take immediately effective action. Instead of being extremely active or absurdly passive, they chose the middle way which of all possible courses turned out to be the most disastrous.

Hoare assumed his new duties with the pleasure of satisfied ambition, but also with some trepidation. To a friend he confided, "India was bad enough, but this—"! The affairs of a world where Japan was triumphant, Mussolini rampant, and Hitler gathering his power for a spring were terribly daunting.

A man of supreme stamina and outstanding qualities would have needed a respite after so much exhausting work, and few would credit Samuel Hoare with belonging to that class. Conscientious, tired, apprehensive, he en-

tered upon the *damnosa hereditas* bequeathed by Simon
without even a chance to revive his limited energies.

Nemesis had clearly marked him down. In mid-September at the Assembly of the League of Nations he was the
mouthpiece of a statement of policy to which several
heads in the Cabinet had made their contribution. This
resounding lecture which Sam Hoare read to the representatives of the member states had a remarkable effect in
England—it electrified a public which had, thanks to a
movement misnamed the "peace ballot," become very
League-minded.

A few months before the League of Nations Union,
under the inspiration of Lord Cecil, had organized a poll
throughout England, Scotland, and Wales. Men and
women over the age of eighteen were asked to answer the
following questions:

(1) Should Great Britain remain a member of the
League of Nations?

(2) Are you in favor of an all-round reduction of armaments *by international agreement?*

(3) Are you in favor of the all-round abolition of national military and naval aircraft *by international agreement?*

(4) Should the manufacture and sale of armaments for
private profit be prohibited *by international agreement?*

(5) Do you consider that if a nation insists on attacking
another the other nations should combine to compel it to
stop by:

(a) economic and nonmilitary measures;

(b) if necessary, military measures?

Eleven million people voluntarily took part in the ballot. Every question received an enormous affirmative vote.
The majority for 5 (b) was less overwhelming than the

rest but was sufficient to show that, in the last resort, plenty of English people would support the firmest action possible.

When Hoare's League speech was composed the Cabinet, who, for reasons which were never very clear, had begun by treating the poll as a veiled "attack upon the government," most certainly had the results of the vote in mind. One particular phrase of Hoare's flattered the public fancy—"steady and collective resistance to all acts of unprovoked aggression." That Hoare himself regarded these words as the heart of his message seems proved by his repeating them at the moment of their delivery with an emphatic descent of the open palm.

But this speech did not shoo off Signor Mussolini. Hostilities began in October. Baldwin, contriving to discern a "lull" (apparently not for the Ethiopians), decided on a general election. With Sam Hoare's noble phrases on their lips, and the delectable personality of Anthony Eden to extol, government candidates collectively won a great victory.

That was in mid-November. Toward the end of that month Sir Samuel, under his doctor's orders, left London for a holiday. He said he was urged to stay in Paris on his way to Switzerland; but some at least of his colleagues in the Cabinet urged him not to pause in his journey.

In Paris Hoare had to discuss the situation with the cunning Laval, who had earlier in the same year made a compact with Mussolini. To Laval the only thing that mattered was the security of France against German aggression. He did not care for the rule of law. With Laval controlling French foreign policy, the long-standing charge that France was interested in the League simply

Sir Samuel Hoare, today Lord Privy Seal, pictured inspecting Chatham Barracks when he was First Sea Lord. He has held many high posts, and is considered one of the shrewdest diplomats of his time. "He is serious and desperately sensitive—he is the soul of care and caution."

as a means of permanently subjecting Germany seemed to acquire a certain colorable justification.

So Laval twisted along between the fancied new security on France's Italian frontier and the ultimate necessity of keeping British friendship. He and Hoare forgot the fine speeches of September, and Hoare in particular overlooked what he and his colleagues had been saying during the general election. They forgot that their duty was supposed to be to discover means of carrying out Article X of the Covenant of the League:

"The Members of the League undertake to respect and preserve as against external aggression the territorial integrity and existing political independence of all Members of the League."

The next logical step in the organizing of collective resistance to aggression was the oil sanction. It would have been effective; Mussolini had proclaimed that he would have treated it as an act of war and would retaliate accordingly. Therefore, said Laval and Hoare, we must have no oil sanction!

Incredible as it may appear, that crude process is hardly an abbreviation of the relevant part of Hoare's later personal explanation in the House of Commons. The offender was in fact to be allowed to decide how much pressure could be applied against him!

So they drew up the Laval-Hoare proposals, which immediately leaked into the Paris press. Huge concessions were to be made to a state after she had flouted the League of which she was a member and had committed the most impudent and flagrant aggression.

When some of Hoare's advisers in Paris heard of the terms they were so amazed that they suggested that the people at home would not stand them. Hoare tartly replied that they knew nothing about it. He then continued his journey to Switzerland and tried to rest.

Now his path may have been strewn with thorns and stones. But he must have had a mental blind spot if he thought public opinion would accept these proposals calmly. You can hardly win an election on one policy and within three weeks expect to be allowed to repudiate it.

It may be asked whether he could have done anything else. If he could contemplate behaving thus in Paris in December, how could he ever have made his September speech at Geneva? He should have found some means of obliging the French government openly to specify the co-operative action they were prepared to undertake. Rather than put his name to the proposals at all he should have resigned. For the public held him to be bound both by the Covenant and by the September speech.

Seldom before or since has a tide of indignation mounted with such overwhelming rapidity. Members of Parliament were deluged with wrathful correspondence. The press joined in the storm. Most decisive of all was the conduct of *The Times*. *The Times* is not an official organ of government policy. That is an error constantly entertained by the foreigner. It is independent; as independent as any section of the free British press. But when a government of the Right is in office it normally gives support, even though such support may periodically impose a strain upon consistency or logic. So, if *The Times* turns upon an individual member or policy of such a government, the man or the cause is in danger of being destroyed.

For one edition *The Times* stuttered, but then the direction of its own awfully respectable circle became so clearly set that it began to thunder out his doom upon Sir Samuel Hoare. The narrow strip of territory proposed to be given to the Ethiopian emperor, Haile Selassie, as a means of access to the sea and as compensation for what he would be losing was satirized in a famous leading article entitled "A corridor for camels."

This was too much; it was too like mutiny within the camp. Indeed, this strange instance of attachment to principle is quite inexplicable when we recall the later periodic prostrations of *The Times* before Mussolini's brother aggressors in Germany.

Hoare had to cut short his holiday and come home. But Nemesis—a warped and unwarranted Nemesis—was filling in every detail in her plan for his discomfiture. Before she let him leave Switzerland she cast him down on the ice and injured his nose; so when next he publicly appeared in London he wore a wide strip of plaster across his face.

Injuries were piling up, though the whole press did not turn and rend him. With an uncanny instinct for backing the losing horse the *Evening Standard* published a placard bearing the charmingly ambiguous legend "Back Sir Samuel Hoare!" When I first saw it I imagined that the word "back" was an imperative and that the proper name was to be parsed in the vocative case, the whole sentence meaning "Away—" or "avaunt—Sir Samuel Hoare!"

Then I recalled that such an interpretation was not consistent with the policy the Beaverbrook press had been urging. They could hardly want Hoare to retire in shame. So I next took the phrase to be an exclamation of surprise, delight and welcome: "So you're back again, Sir Samuel Hoare! We are glad to see you."

Finally it occurred to me that there was a third possibility. The word "back" could certainly be an imperative of the transitive verb which colloquially means "support" and Sir Samuel Hoare was the object. The world was invited to support the coauthor of the Paris proposals.

Hoare resigned. The moment of his speech of personal explanation after his resignation was the first of many dramatic scenes in the life of the Parliament which had been born five weeks before, which saw the abdication of Edward VIII and declaration of war against Germany, and which is still in being.

There were not only the circumstances which many regarded as betrayal. There was also the central figure himself, flushed, ill, gloomy, almost tragically ludicrous with the broad band of plaster disfiguring his sorrowful features. A career of uninteresting but unqualified success was suddenly wrecked after barely half a year at the Foreign Office.

Hoare seemed to know that the word "traitor" was in the minds of some, for he spoke with a brisk directness amounting almost to defiance. There was no sound of the namby-pamby accents which, falling from Hoare's lips, had so often made Morpheus the master of the chamber. He explained that he had been obsessed with the need to avoid a European war, and argued at some length in favor of his proposals.

Great Britain alone, said Hoare, had taken any military precautions. "Not a ship, not a machine, not a man had been moved by any other member state." He might have mentioned the important circumstance that several Mediterranean powers had promised Great Britain the use of their ports in the event of hostilities between Italy and Britain. He protested humbly that his conscience was clear. Only at the very end did his voice falter. He went from the packed chamber to the loneliness outside on the verge of collapse.

For a sick man the speech was a stout effort. Many have said that subsequent events have proved his wisdom. But such apologists overlook the fact that his own action was itself an event of cardinal consequence and may in itself have fatally compromised the future of the League. Aggressive acts and aggressive designs were being rewarded.

The next logical measure of restraint, the oil sanction, was never proceeded with, partly, no doubt, because others besides Hoare feared the consequences of effective action, but probably also because opinion in the United States was disastrously estranged. No more was heard of the willingness of the United States to "limit her supplies of oil to the aggressor state to normal," that is only to allow the customary peacetime stream to flow into Italy, a limitation which would render effective an otherwise general embargo upon oil imports.

In Hoare's mind there must have been an intellectual gap; he had not faced the fact that it is useless to try to restrain a robber if you hand him the swag directly he growls about what he will do to you. As to the complaint about our isolated defensive action, is it too much to say that he should have thought of that before and arranged— or tried to arrange—collective action?

It was a resounding crash. Hoare's own suffering as he was racked by the pangs of his acutely developed ambitions is beyond the power of human imagination. But before many weeks had passed his following were pushing his claims for readmission to the Cabinet. "The Cabinet," they complained, "is not overstocked with brains; however gross some may regard Hoare's error, nobody can deny his ability. Let him return to strengthen the team."

It was made known that a minister would soon be appointed to co-ordinate the defense departments. The problem of defense was debated on March 9, 1936. Though it was less than three months since his resignation, Hoare saw fit to intervene from a back bench.

His contribution was clearly intended to impress with its statesmanlike breadth of vision. But it really meant little except at its peroration, which many found too full of meaning. It was a painfully lavish puff of Baldwin. There were the final words: "Among the prime minister's followers there will be none more willing to give him support than a very old friend and colleague who has just had the privilege of addressing the House this afternoon."

Why, someone asked, did not Hoare say outright, "Please make me minister for co-ordination of defense"? By this obtuse obviousness he destroyed any chance he may have had of being hustled back so soon into office. Neither he nor Winston Churchill was offered the new job. Baldwin's choice fell upon the attorney general, Sir Thomas Inskip.

But Hoare's sad divorce from office ended in June. Lord Monsell, the former chief whip in the House of Commons, smilingly resigned from the Admiralty and Hoare stepped into his boots as first lord. During his term naval rearmament went ahead. He supervised with satisfaction the strengthening of the arm which had in his judgment not been sufficiently powerful at the height of the Italo-Ethiopian trouble.

By the end of the year Baldwin was leaning on the advice of "his old friend and colleague" as Edward VIII was presented with his dreadful dilemma. It was probably sound advice. Hoare watched his old confidant guide the nation over the perilous morass with consummate power and skill.

Neville Chamberlain shares Baldwin's opinion of Hoare, for when he succeeded as premier in May, 1937, Hoare was promoted to the great position of the Home Office. Among other things the home secretary has special charge of the public treatment of crime and the criminal. Again he was successor to Sir John Simon. Men began to wonder if he might someday follow him as chancellor of the exchequer. There is now little else for Hoare to become except prime minister, which would be the goal of his warmly nurtured ambitions.

It is difficult to recall a precedent of a man becoming the head of a government after a setback like Hoare's resignation. Another circumstance recently contributed unkindly to the darkening of his prospects. His zeal was so great that he has been unable to hold his office without proposing a major act of criminal reform.

I have already referred to the Liberal influence in Hoare's composition. To him it is no longer right to base the practice of punishment upon the theory of retribution; its functions must be deterrent and reformative. This principle formed the provisions of the Criminal Justice Bill.

But no one could imagine that this abatement of the rigors of our penal system commanded the joyous approval of the whole of Sir Samuel's party. There are many Conservatives who, rightly or wrongly, identify severity with deterrence.

One of the provisions of the bill is to abolish flogging except for attacks in jail upon prison officers. By a huge majority a conference of Conservative women voted for the retention of flogging. It is pertinent to ask how many had read the report on flogging by a committee, most of whose members had entered the inquiry in a mood favorable to its retention. The committee, after hearing the evidence, unanimously reported in favor of the abolition of flogging. Those women seemed more interested in violent penalties than in reformation and deterrent measures.

The war came and the whole bill had to be abandoned. But the controversy seriously shook Hoare's prestige. It was bad luck, very bad luck. Not all Hoare's other qualifications, birth, brains, career, high connections, Harrovian education, could wholly nullify the resentment at what was so widely regarded as gratuitous interference with a penal system that is already unreasonably lenient. Why, his party asked, must a Conservative home secretary be so provocative? This time there was no Stanley Baldwin at the head of the government to insist on a great reform.

One thing Hoare did *not* do. He did not touch the death penalty. Yet the case is theoretically just as strong for its abolition. One's instinct would incline one to the contrary belief. But the experience of countries that have abolished capital punishment shows that the chair, the gallows, the firing squad, and the ax are less *certain* penalties than long-term imprisonment. Too many guilty men are acquitted. Sometimes an innocent man is executed.

Imprisonment, being less appalling to the minds of juries and therefore more certain in its operation against murderers, is the surer deterrent. In most abolitionist countries, paradoxical though the fact may be, the murder rate has declined when the death penalty has been replaced by imprisonment. Juries, where a verdict of "guilty" may mean the rope, execute flights of fancy to find a man innocent.

These facts were probably well known to Hoare, but there was no sign that he intended to upset the scaffold. But with the arrival of war, the executioner who does not discriminate, Hoare was removed from the Home Office and was called into the Inner Cabinet as a special counselor.

His embittering trials have left their mark upon Samuel Hoare. If appearances ever betray what is revolving in a man's mind he must worry ceaselessly—about his work, his department, and himself. He may not magnetize his companions. But very rarely is such academic excellence to be found within a character so absolutely incorruptible. His theoretical claims to leadership are great and he may suffer bitterly if they are thwarted, just as he suffers unnecessarily when he has politically to make a choice between two evils.

No doubt it pained Hoare, as home secretary, to have to exclude any refugee. He knew well enough that Great Britain would profit eventually as she had profited in the past if she kept her doors open as an asylum for the persecuted. But he knew also that the public would not agree without qualification and that a too-ready greeting might promote such anti-Semitism as already existed in Britain. That emotion is nearly absent from the mass of the British people. But Hoare is essentially a cautious man, prone to make haste slowly and to avoid unnecessary risks. If the war lasts the three years that the government officially deems possible, the value of Hoare's patience may be above rubies.